Letter Home

Viewing and Drawing 3-D

Date: _____

Dear Family Member:

Your child is studying the geometry of three-dimensional objects such as boxes, cubes, and objects made with building blocks. Students will take on the role of toy designers and apply their knowledge of geometry to drawing plans for toys and small buildings.

You can help at home.

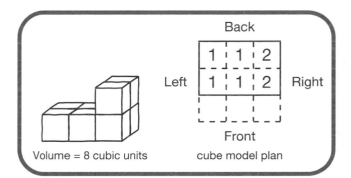

Students find the volume of cube models and describe them using cube model plans.

- Please save empty tissue and cereal boxes and send them to school with your child. We need them by _____.

- In a few days, ask your child to show you the faces, edges, and vertices (corners) of a tissue or cereal box. Ask him or her to describe the shapes, lines, and angles that form the box. Through the descriptions, he or she is using the language of geometry.

- Ask your child to build a tower or other shape with toy blocks or cubes. Later in the unit, ask him or her how to describe this shape using cube model plans.

- Help your child practice the multiplication facts for the square numbers using the *Triangle Flash Cards*.

Thank you for being interested in your child's mathematics education. By exploring math with your child, you are making math a part of your child's everyday world.

Sincerely,

_____

Carta al hogar

Mirando y dibujando en tres dimensiones

Fecha: _____

Estimado miembro de familia:

Su hijo/a está estudiando la geometría de objetos tridimensionales como cajas, cubos y objetos hechos con bloques. Los estudiantes harán el papel de diseñadores de juguetes y aplicarán sus conocimientos de geometría para dibujar planos para juguetes y edificios pequeños.

Usted puede ayudar en casa.

Volumen = 8 unidades cúbicas   plano de modelo cubos

Los estudiantes hallan el volumen de modelos de cubos y los describen usando planos de modelos de cubos.

- Guarde las cajas vacías de pañuelos de papel y de cereal y déselas a su hijo/a para que las traiga a la escuela. Las necesitamos para el día _____.

- Dentro de unos días, pídale a su hijo/a que le muestre las caras, las aristas (los bordes) y los vértices (las esquinas) de una caja de pañuelos de papel o de cereal. Pídale que describa las figuras, las rectas y los ángulos que forman la caja. Al hacer las descripciones, su hijo/a practicará el lenguaje geométrico.

- Pídale a su hijo/a que construya una torre u otra figura con bloques o cubos de juguete. Más adelante en la unidad, pregúntele cómo describiría esta figura usando planos de modelos de cubos.

- Ayude a su hijo/a a practicar las tablas de multiplicación con números cuadrados usando las tarjetas triangulares.

Gracias por su interés en la educación matemática de su hijo/a. Al explorar las matemáticas junto a su hijo/a, usted está ayudando a que las matemáticas sean parte de la vida cotidiana de su hijo/a.

Atentamente,

_____

Unit Resource Guide
Unit 18

Viewing and Drawing 3-D

THIRD EDITION

KENDALL/HUNT PUBLISHING COMPANY
4050 Westmark Drive   Dubuque, Iowa   52002

A TIMS® Curriculum
University of Illinois at Chicago

UIC The University of Illinois
at Chicago

The original edition was based on work supported by the National Science Foundation under grant No. MDR 9050226 and the University of Illinois at Chicago. Any opinions, findings, and conclusions or recommendations expressed in this publication are those of the author(s) and do not necessarily reflect the views of the granting agencies.

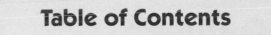

Table of Contents

Unit 18
Viewing and Drawing 3-D

Outline 2

Background 8

Observational Assessment Record 11

Daily Practice and Problems 13

Lesson 1 *Viewing 3-D Objects* 21

Lesson 2 *Drawing 3-D Objects* 33

Lesson 3 *Building and Planning Cube Models* 46

Lesson 4 *Top, Front, and Right Side Views* 59

Lesson 5 *Problems with Shapes* 73

Home Practice Answer Key 79

Glossary 81

Unit 18

Outline
Viewing and Drawing 3-D

Unit Summary

Estimated Class Sessions
6

In this unit students visualize and describe three-dimensional objects. They describe three-dimensional objects (e.g., rectangular prisms and objects made with connecting cubes) in words by talking about the faces, edges, and vertices (corners). They gather information about three-dimensional objects (cube models) by measuring and recording the height, volume, and area of the base. They also use three methods to represent three-dimensional shapes in two dimensions: sketching cubes and other boxes, making cube model plans, and recording three views of the cube models—the top, front, and right side views. The DPP for this unit provides practice with and assesses the multiplication facts for the square numbers.

Major Concept Focus

- multiple representations of shapes
- three-dimensional objects
- cubes and rectangular prisms
- drawing cubes and rectangular prisms
- edges
- faces
- vertices
- cube models
- cube model plans
- area
- length
- volume
- multiple solution strategies
- practice and assessment of the multiplication facts for the square numbers

Assessment Indicators

Use the following Assessment Indicators and the *Observational Assessment Record* that follows the Background section in this unit to assess students on key ideas.

A1. Can students identify the faces, edges, and vertices of a box (rectangular prism)?

A2. Can students find the area of the base, height, and volume of cube models?

A3. Can students translate between a model, its cube model plan, and a three-dimensional drawing?

A4. Can students describe the top, front, and right side views of a cube model?

A5. Do students demonstrate fluency with the multiplication facts for the square numbers?

Unit Planner

	Lesson Information	Supplies	Copies/Transparencies
Lesson 1 **Viewing 3-D Objects** URG Pages 21–32 SG Pages 266–269 DPP A–B HP Part 1 *Estimated Class Sessions* **1**	**Activity** Students view boxes from different perspectives and describe what they see. They compare 3-D objects to 2-D drawings of the objects. **Math Facts** DPP items A and B provide practice with the multiplication facts for the square numbers. **Homework** 1. For homework students collect drawings or pictures of boxes, paste the pictures on paper, trace the edges of each box, and record the number of faces and edges seen. 2. Assign Part 1 of the Home Practice. 3. Students study the multiplication facts for the square numbers using *Triangle Flash Cards*.	• 1 empty tissue box or box of similar size and shape per student pair and 1 for the teacher • Mr. Origin	• 1 copy of *Triangle Flash Cards: Square Numbers* URG Page 30 per student, optional
Lesson 2 **Drawing 3-D Objects** URG Pages 33–45 SG Pages 270–272 DAB Pages 263–265 DPP C–D HP Part 2 *Estimated Class Sessions* **1**	**Activity** Students compare a 2-D drawing of a cube to an actual 3-D cube. After comparing and describing faces, edges, parallel lines, and shapes, students draw cubes and other rectangular prisms (boxes). **Homework** 1. Students draw a box at home for homework. 2. Students complete the Journal Prompt at home. 3. Assign Part 2 of the Home Practice. **Assessment** As an assessment, students draw a rectangular prism using a box or other classroom object as a model.	• 1 cube (e.g. connecting cube or base-ten piece) per student • 1 large cube (e.g. large base-ten piece or cardboard box) • 1 empty cereal box per student pair • 3 different colored pens or pencils per student • 1 ruler per student • masking tape or self-adhesive notes, optional • 12 toothpicks per student and 12 for the teacher, optional • 8 miniature marshmallows per student and 8 for the teacher, optional • 3 blue pattern blocks per student, optional • 3 overhead blue pattern blocks, optional	

	Lesson Information	Supplies	Copies/ Transparencies
Lesson 3 **Building and Planning Cube Models** URG Pages 46–58 SG Pages 273–276 DPP E–F HP Part 3 *Estimated Class Sessions* **1**	**Activity** Students build and describe cube models using 2-D representations called cube model plans. Students use cube model plans to determine the area of a cube model's base, its volume, and its height. Given specifications, students build cube models and, in the process, solve problems with multiple solutions. **Math Facts** DPP Bit E provides practice with multiplication facts for the square numbers. **Homework** Assign Part 3 of the Home Practice. **Assessment** Use the *Observational Assessment Record* to record students' abilities to translate between a cube model, its cube model plan, and a drawing.	• 30 connecting cubes per student pair	• 3 copies of *3 × 3 Cube Model Plans* URG Page 55 per student • 1 transparency of *3 × 3 Cube Model Plans* URG Page 55, optional • 1 transparency of *Dee's Cube Model Plan* URG Page 56 • 1 copy of *Observational Assessment Record* URG Pages 11–12 to be used throughout this unit
Lesson 4 **Top, Front, and Right Side Views** URG Pages 59–72 SG Pages 277–281 DPP G–J HP Part 4 *Estimated Class Sessions* **2**	**Activity** Students view cube models from the top, front, and right side and then record these three views. Students also solve puzzles about cube models. **Math Facts** DPP item G provides computation and mental math practice. Bit I provides practice with the multiplication facts for the square numbers. **Homework** 1. Assign the *Three Ways to Show 3-D Models* Assessment Pages either for homework or in-class assessment. 2. Assign Home Practice Part 4. **Assessment** 1. Students complete the *Three Ways to Show 3-D Models* Assessment Blackline Masters. 2. Use the *Observational Assessment Record* to record students' abilities to identify the front, right, and top views of a cube model.	• 30 connecting cubes per student • masking tape, optional	• 2 copies of *3 × 3 Cube Model Plans* URG Page 55 per student • 2 copies of *Three-view Records* URG Page 69 per student • 1 copy of *Three Ways to Show 3-D Models* URG Pages 67–68 per student
Lesson 5 **Problems with Shapes** URG Pages 73–78 SG Pages 282–283 DPP K–L *Estimated Class Sessions* **1**	**Activity** Students solve a set of word problems involving geometric concepts. **Math Facts** DPP Bit K is the multiplication quiz on the square numbers. **Homework** Assign some or all of the problems for homework. **Assessment** 1. Students complete DPP item K Multiplication Quiz: Squares. 2. Use the *Observational Assessment Record* to document students' abilities to find the area of the base, height, and volume of a cube model.	• 20 connecting cubes per student • crayons or colored pencils	• 1 copy of *3 × 3 Cube Model Plans* URG Page 55 per student • 1 copy of *Individual Assessment Record Sheet* TIG Assessment section per student, previously copied for use throughout the year.

(Continued)

Lesson Information	Supplies	Copies/Transparencies
3. Transfer appropriate documentation from the Unit 18 *Observational Assessment Record* to students' *Individual Assessment Record Sheets*.		

Connections

A current list of literature and software connections is available at *www.mathtrailblazers.com*. You can also find information on connections in the *Teacher Implementation Guide* Literature List and Software List sections.

Literature Connections

Suggested Titles

- Adkins, Jan. *How a House Happens*. Walker and Company, Inc., New York, 1972. (Lesson 4)

Software Connections

- *Make A Map 3D* develops map reading and direction skills.
- *Math Arena* is a collection of math activities that reinforces many math concepts.
- *Building Perspective Deluxe* develops spatial reasoning and visual thinking in three dimensions.
- *MicroWorlds EX* is a drawing program that helps students develop spatial reasoning and an understanding of coordinates while making shapes.
- *Mighty Math Calculating Crew* poses short answer questions about three-dimensional shapes.

Teaching All Math Trailblazers Students

Math Trailblazers® lessons are designed for students with a wide range of abilities. The lessons are flexible and do not require significant adaptation for diverse learning styles or academic levels. However, when needed, lessons can be tailored to allow students to engage their abilities to the greatest extent possible while building knowledge and skills.

To assist you in meeting the needs of all students in your classroom, this section contains information about some of the features in the curriculum that allow all students access to mathematics. For additional information, see the Teaching the *Math Trailblazers* Student: Meeting Individual Needs section in the *Teacher Implementation Guide.*

Differentiation Opportunities in this Unit

Journal Prompts

Journal prompts provide opportunities for students to explain and reflect on mathematical problems. They can help both students who need practice explaining their ideas and students who benefit from answering higher order questions. Students with various learning styles can express themselves using pictures, words, and sentences. Teachers can alter journal prompts to suit students' ability levels. The following lesson contains a journal prompt:

- Lesson 2 *Drawing 3-D Objects*

DPP Challenges

DPP Challenges are items from the Daily Practice and Problems that usually take more than fifteen minutes to complete. These problems are more thought-provoking and can be used to stretch students' problem-solving skills. The following lessons have a DPP Challenge in them:

- DPP Challenge D from Lesson 2 *Drawing 3-D Objects*
- DPP Challenge F from Lesson 3 *Building and Planning Cube Models*

Extensions

Use extensions to enrich lessons. Many extensions provide opportunities to further involve or challenge students of all abilities. Take a moment to review the extensions prior to beginning this unit. Some extensions may require additional preparation and planning. The following lessons contain extensions:

- Lesson 2 *Drawing 3-D Objects*
- Lesson 3 *Building and Planning Cube Models*
- Lesson 4 *Top, Front, and Right Side Views*

Background
Viewing and Drawing 3-D

This unit deals with visualizing and describing three-dimensional objects. Our study is restricted to simple objects: rectangular prisms (boxes) and objects made with connecting cubes.

When looking at a box, what do you see from different points of view? For example, although we know that a cube has six square faces, we can see at most three faces at a time. When we hold a cube so that we see only one face, we see that face as a square. However, when we hold a cube so that we can see two or three faces at one time, the faces may look like parallelograms (or another quadrilateral). Therefore, when describing or drawing three-dimensional objects, we must reconcile what we know about these objects to what we see when we view them from different perspectives.

viewing one cube face   viewing three cube faces

Figure 1: *The number of faces seen depends on perspective.*

The challenge to students in this unit is to represent three-dimensional (3-D) objects on paper and to interpret such representations. Students describe three-dimensional objects in words by talking about the faces, edges, and vertices (corners). They give information about three-dimensional objects by measuring and recording the height, volume, and area of the faces. They also use three methods to represent three-dimensional shapes in two dimensions: sketching cubes and other boxes, making

cube model plans, and recording three views. Figure 2 provides an example of each method.

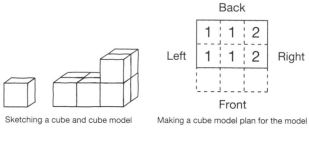

Sketching a cube and cube model   Making a cube model plan for the model

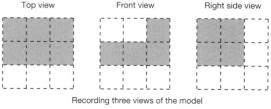

Recording three views of the model

Figure 2: *Two-dimensional representations of a three-dimensional object*

Dimensions

In Grades 1 and 2 of this curriculum and in Unit 8 *Mapping and Coordinates*, students used Mr. Origin to represent the origin as they located objects using a coordinate system, such as a map. We can also use Mr. Origin to help understand dimensions. A line is one-dimensional since we need only *one* number, or coordinate, to locate a point on the line with respect to the origin. In Figure 3, each point is located by giving its left/right distance from the origin. For example, the spool is 20 cm to the left of the origin.

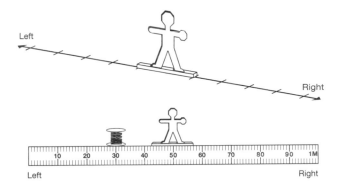

Figure 3: *Using one coordinate to locate a point on a one-dimensional line*

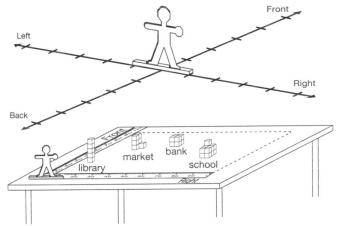

Figure 4: *Using two coordinates to locate a point on a two-dimensional map*

Similarly, a flat surface is two-dimensional since we can determine the location of any point by choosing an origin (Mr. Origin) and specifying *two* coordinates. Locating a building on the model city in Figure 4 requires two coordinates: one that gives the distance of the building to the right of Mr. Origin and one that gives the distance in front of Mr. Origin. For example, the coordinates of the bank, with respect to Mr. Origin, are approximately 52 cm right and 67 cm front. (If the origin were in the center of the map, the two coordinates could be given in terms of left/right and front/back.)

Although we generally think of two-dimensional objects as flat, the surface of the Earth is an example of a curved two-dimensional surface. We use two numbers—latitude and longitude—to determine the location of any point on the surface of the Earth.

Real-world objects are three-dimensional. The house shown in Figure 5 is just one example. If Mr. Origin stands at the intersection of the three axes to represent the origin, we can locate the bug inside the house using three coordinates (left/right, front/back, and up/down).

Students explore all three dimensions as they plan, build, sketch, and measure cube models. These activities provide opportunities for describing geometric attributes such as vertices, edges, and faces. Using geometry, they learn different ways to represent three-dimensional objects in two dimensions on paper.

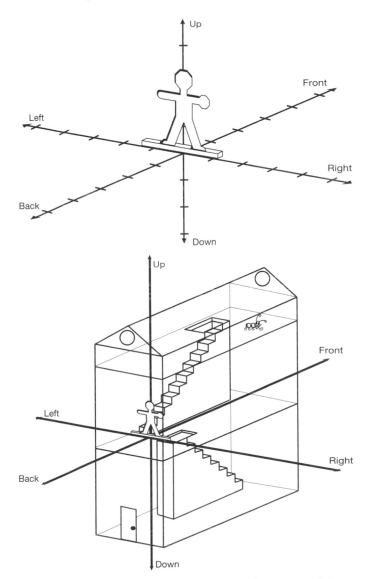

Figure 5: *Using three coordinates to locate a point in a three-dimensional object*

Observational Assessment Record

A1 Can students identify the faces, edges, and vertices of a box (rectangular prism)?

A2 Can students find the area of the base, height, and volume of cube models?

A3 Can students translate between a model, its cube model plan, and a three-dimensional drawing?

A4 Can students describe the top, front, and right side views of a cube model?

A5 Do students demonstrate fluency with the multiplication facts for the square numbers?

A6 _____

Name	A1	A2	A3	A4	A5	A6	Comments
1.							
2.							
3.							
4.							
5.							
6.							
7.							
8.							
9.							
10.							
11.							
12.							
13.							

Name	A1	A2	A3	A4	A5	A6	Comments
14.							
15.							
16.							
17.							
18.							
19.							
20.							
21.							
22.							
23.							
24.							
25.							
26.							
27.							
28.							
29.							
30.							
31.							
32.							

Unit 18

Daily Practice and Problems
Viewing and Drawing 3-D

A DPP Menu for Unit 18

Two Daily Practice and Problems (DPP) items are included for each class session listed in the Unit Outline. A scope and sequence chart for the DPP is in the *Teacher Implementation Guide*.

Icons in the Teacher Notes column designate the subject matter of each DPP item. The first item in each class session is always a Bit and the second is either a Task or Challenge. Each item falls into one or more of the categories listed below. A menu of the DPP items for Unit 18 follows.

N Number Sense	Computation	Time	Geometry
C, D, F–J	C, G, H, J, L	L	B
Math Facts	$ Money	Measurement	Data
A, B, E, G, I, K	D	B, F	

Practicing and Assessing the Multiplication Facts

In Unit 11, students began the systematic, strategies-based study of the multiplication facts. In Unit 18, students review and practice the multiplication facts for the square numbers. The *Triangle Flash Cards* for this group were distributed in Unit 13 in the *Discovery Assignment Book* immediately following the Home Practice. They also are in Lesson 1. In Unit 18, DPP items A, B, E, and I provide practice with multiplication facts for this group. Bit K is the Multiplication Quiz: Squares.

For information on the distribution and study of the multiplication facts in Grade 3, see the DPP Guides for Units 3 and 11. For a detailed explanation of our approach to learning and assessing the math facts in Grade 3 see the *Grade 3 Facts Resource Guide* and for information for Grades K–5, see the TIMS Tutor: *Math Facts* in the *Teacher Implementation Guide*.

Students may solve the items individually, in groups, or as a class. The items may also be assigned for homework. The DPPs are also available on the Teacher Resource CD.

Student Questions	Teacher Notes

A Multiplication: Squares

Do these problems in your head. Write only the answers.

A. $6 \times 6 =$

B. $5 \times 5 =$

C. $2 \times 2 =$

D. $9 \times 9 =$

E. $7 \times 7 =$

F. $3 \times 3 =$

G. $4 \times 4 =$

H. $8 \times 8 =$

I. $10 \times 10 =$

J. $1 \times 1 =$

TIMS Bit $\frac{5}{\times 7}$

Discuss strategies with students. Tell students to practice the multiplication facts for the square numbers at home using the *Triangle Flash Cards*. The flash cards for this group were distributed in Unit 13 in the *Discovery Assignment Book* following the Home Practice. The cards are also in Lesson 1. Advise students when you will give the quiz on the square numbers. Bit K is a quiz on these facts.

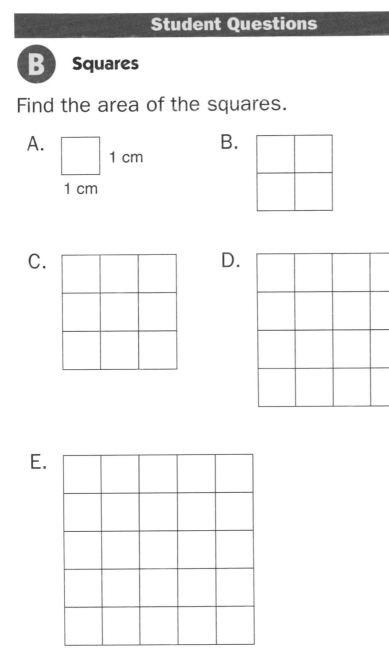

B **Squares**

Find the area of the squares.

A.   1 cm
1 cm

B.

C.

D.

E.

F. What is the area of a 6 cm × 6 cm square?

G. What is the area of a 7 cm × 7 cm square?

H. Why do we call the square numbers *square numbers?* Give an example.

TIMS Task

A. 1 sq cm

B. 4 sq cm

C. 9 sq cm

D. 16 sq cm

E. 25 sq cm

F. 36 sq cm

G. 49 sq cm

H. Possible response: 25 is a square number because 5 × 5 = 25. You can multiply 5 times itself and get 25. The area of a square that has sides equal to 5 cm is 25 sq cm.

C Addition and Subtraction Practice

Complete these problems using pencil and paper or mental math to find the answers.

1. Predict which of the following problems will have the smallest answer (sum or difference).

2.
$$
\begin{array}{r} 750 \\ -262 \end{array}
$$
3.
$$
\begin{array}{r} 689 \\ +851 \end{array}
$$
4.
$$
\begin{array}{r} 148 \\ +198 \end{array}
$$
5.
$$
\begin{array}{r} 9145 \\ -8997 \end{array}
$$

TIMS Bit

1. Discuss students' predictions and strategies for finding the smallest answer before solving the problem.

2. 488

3. 1540

4. 346

5. 148

D Coin Fractions

1. Complete the following table:

Name of Coin	Value of Coin (in $)	Fraction of Dollar
penny	$.01	$\frac{1}{100}$
nickel		
dime		
quarter		
half-dollar		
silver dollar		

2. How do you think the quarter and half-dollar got their names?

TIMS Challenge

1.

Coin	Value	Fraction
penny	$.01	$\frac{1}{100}$
nickel	$.05	$\frac{5}{100}$
dime	$.10	$\frac{10}{100}$
quarter	$.25	$\frac{25}{100}$
half-dollar	$.50	$\frac{50}{100}$
silver dollar	$1.00	$\frac{100}{100}$

Discourage students from writing $.01¢.

2. A quarter is $\frac{1}{4}$ or a quarter of a dollar. A half-dollar is 50 cents out of 100 cents or $\frac{1}{2}$ of a dollar.

Student Questions	Teacher Notes

E **Story Solving**

Write a story and draw a picture about 8×8. Write a number sentence for your picture.

TIMS Bit ⬛

Discuss students' stories with the class.

F **Containers**

Suppose you have one empty container that holds exactly 5 quarts and another empty container that holds exactly 2 quarts. Figure out a way to measure exactly 1 quart of water by pouring water between the containers. You can use as much water from the faucet as you wish.

TIMS Challenge Ⓝ ⚖

Answers may vary. One possible solution: Fill the 2 quart container three times. Each time, empty it into the 5-quart container without overflowing. There will be one quart left in the 2-quart container. Another way: Fill the 5-quart container and empty out 2 quarts. Then, empty out 2 quarts more. One quart is left.

G **Quick Addition**

Do these problems in your head. Write only the answers.

1. $5 + 6 =$

2. $50 + 60 =$

3. $60 + 40 =$

4. $60 + 30 =$

5. $40 + 70 =$

6. $20 + 80 =$

TIMS Bit ⬛ Ⓝ ⬛

1. 11   2. 110
3. 100   4. 90
5. 110   6. 100

These problems provide an opportunity for students to review a few addition facts and to relate them to adding multiples of 10.

Student Questions	Teacher Notes

H **Joe and Moe Smart**

Joe Smart's answer for the problem 19 × 6 was 126. Moe Smart got a different answer. Joe said, "Well, first I did 20 × 6." Moe said, "I agree with that but . . ."

1. Finish Moe's statement explaining to Joe what he did wrong.

2. Tell how you can find 29 × 3.

TIMS Task N ▨

This task serves as an introduction to item J. Students may need to use base-ten pieces to do the problem. Afterwards, however, discuss how these problems can be done mentally using multiples of 10.

1. Your answer should be less than 120 since 19 × 6 will be less than 20 × 6. Subtract 6 from 120 and get 114.

2. Two of many possible solutions:

   A. 30 × 3 = 90;
   90 − 3 = 87 or

   B. 20 × 3 = 60;
   9 × 3 = 27;
   60 + 27 = 87

I **More Squares**

For each problem the numbers in the squares must be the same.

A. 64 = ☐ × ☐

B. 36 = ☐ × ☐

C. 9 = ☐ × ☐

D. 25 = ☐ × ☐

E. 49 = ☐ × ☐

F. 81 = ☐ × ☐

G. 100 = ☐ × ☐

H. 16 = ☐ × ☐

I. 4 = ☐ × ☐

J. 1 = ☐ × ☐

TIMS Bit ⁵x̄⁷ N

A. 8

B. 6

C. 3

D. 5

E. 7

F. 9

G. 10

H. 4

I. 2

J. 1

Student Questions	Teacher Notes

J Multiplication

A. $3 \times 25 =$

B. $3 \times 24 =$

C. $3 \times 26 =$

D. $5 \times 30 =$

E. $5 \times 29 =$

F. $5 \times 31 =$

G. $4 \times 50 =$

H. $4 \times 49 =$

I. $4 \times 59 =$

TIMS Task

Discuss students' strategies. Possible strategies are shown below.

A. 75

B. $(3 \times 25) - (3 \times 1) =$
$75 - 3 = 72$

C. $(3 \times 25) + (3 \times 1) =$
$75 + 3 = 78$

D. 150

E. $150 - 5 = 145$

F. $150 + 5 = 155$

G. 200

H. $200 - 4 = 196$

I. $(4 \times 60) - (4 \times 1) =$
$240 - 4 = 236$

K Multiplication Quiz: Squares

Do these problems in your head. Write only the answers.

A. $5 \times 5 =$

B. $4 \times 4 =$

C. $9 \times 9 =$

D. $7 \times 7 =$

E. $10 \times 10 =$

F. $8 \times 8 =$

G. $3 \times 3 =$

H. $1 \times 1 =$

I. $6 \times 6 =$

J. $2 \times 2 =$

TIMS Bit

This quiz is on the squares. We recommend 1 minute for this quiz. Allow students to change pens or pencils after this time is up and complete the remaining problems in a different color. After students take the quiz, have them update their *Multiplication Facts I Know charts*.

L Count on Reading

Ms. Ropel's class read for a total of 778 minutes. Mrs. Cob's class read for 976 minutes.

1. How many more minutes did Mrs. Cob's class read than Ms. Ropel's?

2. A. Did Mrs. Cob's class read for longer than ten hours?

   B. Explain how you can change the answer to Question 1 to hours and minutes.

3. How many minutes altogether did the two classes read?

TIMS Task

1. You may wish to encourage students to try this problem in their head. If the problem were $976 - 776$ the answer would be 200. Subtract 2 more to get 198 minutes.

2. A. Yes; ten hours is 10×60 minutes = 600 minutes. Ms. Cob's class read for 976 minutes.

   B. $60 + 60 + 60 = 180$ minutes or 3 hours; $198 - 180 = 18$ min.; 3 hours and 18 minutes

3. 1754 minutes

Lesson 1

Viewing 3-D Objects

Lesson Overview

Estimated Class Sessions

1

Students view boxes from different perspectives and describe what they see. Students also compare an actual three-dimensional object, a tissue box, to drawings of the box. As they discuss the object and the drawing, they use vocabulary necessary to describe three-dimensional (3-D) and two-dimensional (2-D) shapes.

Key Content

- Describing three-dimensional objects from different perspectives.
- Naming and identifying parts of a rectangular prism (edges, faces, vertices).
- Translating between a rectangular prism and its drawing.

Key Vocabulary

- corner
- edge
- face
- one-dimensional
- rectangular prism
- three-dimensional
- two-dimensional
- vertex, vertices

Math Facts

DPP items A and B provide practice with the multiplication facts for the square numbers.

Homework

1. For homework students collect drawings or pictures of boxes, paste the pictures on paper, trace the edges of each box, and record the number of faces and edges seen.
2. Assign Part 1 of the Home Practice.
3. Students study the multiplication facts for the square numbers using *Triangle Flash Cards*.

Curriculum Sequence

Directions and Coordinates

In Grade 1 Unit 19 *Measurement and Mapping* and Grade 2 Unit 18 *Mapping the Rain Forest,* students were introduced to the directions front/back, left/right, and above/below relative to Mr. Origin. They located objects on a flat surface using coordinates in Grade 3 Unit 8 *Mapping and Coordinates*.

Prisms

Students investigated three-dimensional shapes, including rectangular prisms in Grade 2 Unit 17 *Investigating 3-D Shapes*.

Students will continue working with three-dimensional shapes in Grade 4 Unit 9 *Shapes and Solids*.

Materials List

Supplies and Copies

Student	Teacher
Supplies for Each Student Pair • empty tissue box or box of similar size and shape	**Supplies** • empty tissue box or box of similar size and shape • Mr. Origin
Copies • 1 copy of *Triangle Flash Cards*: *Square Numbers* per student, optional (*Unit Resource Guide* Page 30)	**Copies/Transparencies**

All blackline masters including assessment, transparency, and DPP masters are also on the Teacher Resource CD.

Student Books
Viewing 3-D Objects (*Student Guide* Pages 266–269)

Daily Practice and Problems and Home Practice
DPP items A–B (*Unit Resource Guide* Pages 14–15)
Home Practice Part 1 (*Discovery Assignment Book* Page 260)

Note: Classrooms whose pacing differs significantly from the suggested pacing of the units should use the Math Facts Calendar in Section 4 of the *Facts Resource Guide* to ensure students receive the complete math facts program.

Daily Practice and Problems

Suggestions for using the DPPs are on page 28.

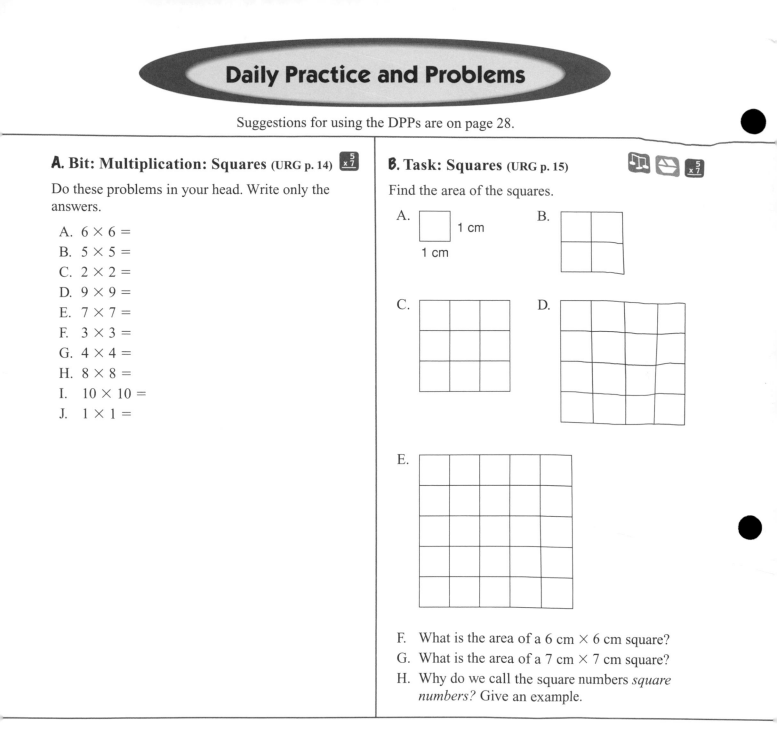

A. Bit: Multiplication: Squares (URG p. 14) $\boxed{\frac{5}{\times 7}}$

Do these problems in your head. Write only the answers.

A. $6 \times 6 =$

B. $5 \times 5 =$

C. $2 \times 2 =$

D. $9 \times 9 =$

E. $7 \times 7 =$

F. $3 \times 3 =$

G. $4 \times 4 =$

H. $8 \times 8 =$

I. $10 \times 10 =$

J. $1 \times 1 =$

B. Task: Squares (URG p. 15)

Find the area of the squares.

A. □ 1 cm

1 cm

B.

C.

D.

E.

F. What is the area of a 6 cm $\times$ 6 cm square?

G. What is the area of a 7 cm $\times$ 7 cm square?

H. Why do we call the square numbers *square numbers?* Give an example.

Part 1 Three Dimensions

Your students might wonder why three-dimensional objects are called three-dimensional. Explain this by referring back to Unit 8 *Mapping and Coordinates*. The short explanation is that we need one coordinate to locate an object on a line (relative to the origin), two coordinates to locate an object on a flat surface, and three coordinates to locate an object in space.

The *Viewing 3-D Objects* Activity Pages in the *Student Guide* introduce students to the terms **one-, two-,** and **three-dimensional** objects using Mr. Origin. Before reading these pages with the class, review what students already know about Mr. Origin. Ask:

- *Which hand is Mr. Origin's right hand?* (the one with the mitten)
- *Which side is his front side?* (The button indicates Mr. Origin's front.)

Place Mr. Origin on the edge of a student's desk with his base parallel to the edge. Place a small object such as an eraser on the edge as well. Then say:

- *Let's say Mr. Origin is stuck on the edge of your desk. How would you describe where the eraser is in relation to Mr. Origin?* (The eraser is to the right or left of Mr. Origin.)

Next, place Mr. Origin on the floor. Remind the students of the class treasure hunt in *Meet Mr. Origin* (Unit 8 Lesson 1). Say:

- *Let's imagine the eraser is our treasure and let's "bury" it somewhere in the classroom by placing it on the floor. How would you describe where the eraser is in relation to Mr. Origin?* (The object is in front of or in back of Mr. Origin. It is also to Mr. Origin's left or right.)
- *How many directions would you have to give?* (You would need to give two directions. For example, the eraser is 150 cm to the left and 210 cm in front of Mr. Origin. That is why we call a flat surface, like a floor or a desk two-dimensional—because we need to give two distances and directions, or dimensions to locate an object.)

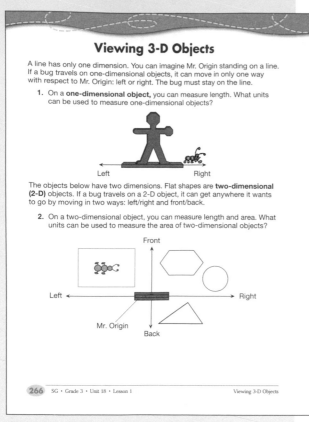

Viewing 3-D Objects

A line has only one dimension. You can imagine Mr. Origin standing on a line. If a bug travels on one-dimensional objects, it can move in only one way with respect to Mr. Origin: left or right. The bug must stay on the line.

1. On a **one-dimensional object,** you can measure length. What units can be used to measure one-dimensional objects?

Left — Right

The objects below have two dimensions. Flat shapes are **two-dimensional (2-D)** objects. If a bug travels on a 2-D object, it can get anywhere it wants to go by moving in two ways: left/right and front/back.

2. On a two-dimensional object, you can measure length and area. What units can be used to measure the area of two-dimensional objects?

Front

Left ← → Right

Mr. Origin

Back

266   SG • Grade 3 • Unit 18 • Lesson 1   Viewing 3-D Objects

Student Guide - page 266 *(Answers on p. 31)*

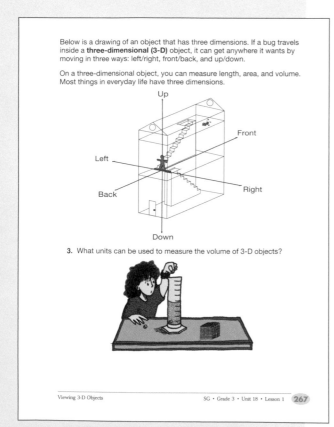

Below is a drawing of an object that has three dimensions. If a bug travels inside a **three-dimensional (3-D)** object, it can get anywhere it wants by moving in three ways: left/right, front/back, and up/down.

On a three-dimensional object, you can measure length, area, and volume. Most things in everyday life have three dimensions.

Up

Front

Left

Back

Right

Down

3. What units can be used to measure the volume of 3-D objects?

Viewing 3-D Objects   SG • Grade 3 • Unit 18 • Lesson 1   267

Student Guide - page 267 *(Answers on p. 31)*

- *Imagine we can hide our treasure anywhere in the room, for example, on the light fixture or in a hole three meters into the ground. How could you describe exactly where the treasure is, including how high or low it is?* (The object is a certain distance above or below Mr. Origin, a certain distance to his right or left, and a certain distance in front of or behind Mr. Origin.)

- *How many directions would you use to describe where something is in relationship to Mr. Origin?* (three)

Read and discuss the first two pages of the *Viewing 3-D Objects* Activity Pages. These pages discuss one-, two-, and three-dimensional shapes. ***Questions 1–3*** ask which units can be used to measure length (one-dimensional shapes), area (two-dimensional shapes), and volume (three-dimensional shapes). To measure length, units such as centimeters, inches, feet, and meters may be used. Square centimeters, square inches, square feet, square meters, and other square units are used to measure area. Cubic units, such as cubic centimeters, cubic inches, cubic feet, and cubic meters, are units used to measure volume.

Part 2 Looking at and Describing Boxes

Students will look at and describe boxes. Children who had this curriculum in second grade have already been introduced to the term **rectangular prism.** A tissue box, a cereal box, and most other boxes are good examples of rectangular prisms. Use the term as appropriate in class discussion. It is not a goal of this lesson for students to define a rectangular prism, but rather to be able to describe a prism as seen from different perspectives.

To complete ***Question 4,*** students count the number of faces, edges, and vertices (corners) on an actual tissue box.

Question 5 asks students how they held the box in order to see one, two, and three faces. If a student can perform a requested action but has trouble explaining it in words, have the child demonstrate what he or she did for the class. Then other students may help him or her describe the action in words. For ***Question 5A,*** for example, a student may say, "I stood up and looked at the top face from directly above it." Encourage the use of mathematical terms such as rectangle, face, edge, and corner or vertex.

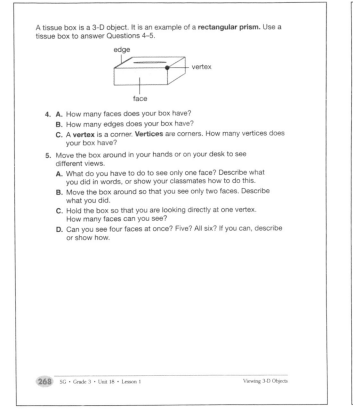

A tissue box is a 3-D object. It is an example of a **rectangular prism**. Use a tissue box to answer Questions 4–5.

4. **A.** How many faces does your box have?
   B. How many edges does your box have?
   C. A **vertex** is a corner. **Vertices** are corners. How many vertices does your box have?

5. Move the box around in your hands or on your desk to see different views.
   A. What do you have to do to see only one face? Describe what you did in words, or show your classmates how to do this.
   B. Move the box around so that you see only two faces. Describe what you did.
   C. Hold the box so that you are looking directly at one vertex. How many faces can you see?
   D. Can you see four faces at once? Five? All six? If you can, describe or show how.

Student Guide - page 268 (Answers on p. 31)

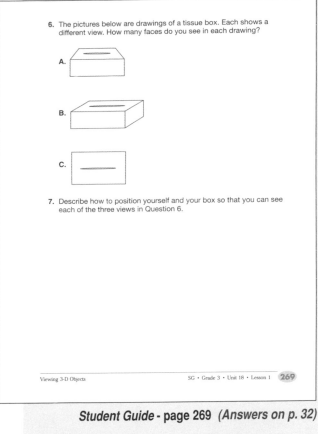

6. The pictures below are drawings of a tissue box. Each shows a different view. How many faces do you see in each drawing?

   A.

   B.

   C.

7. Describe how to position yourself and your box so that you can see each of the three views in Question 6.

Student Guide - page 269 (Answers on p. 32)

Question 5C suggests that a child look "directly at one vertex," enabling him or her to see three faces. If students pick up the box and point a corner directly at their noses, they should be able to do this. In response to *Question 5D,* students may say they can see four, five, or six faces at one time. This is true only if we allow students to disassemble the box or use a mirror. If students offer such solutions, congratulate them on their thinking, but then rephrase the question:

- *Without changing the box or using a mirror, can you see more than three faces at one time?* (No)

Ask students to compare the number of faces, edges, and vertices on the actual box to the number they can see in the pictures in *Question 6.* Comparing an actual box to a picture of the box will help students in the next lesson *Drawing 3-D Objects.*

Content Note

Everyday Words for Naming the Dimensions of 3-D Objects. Height is the label most often used to describe the "up/down" dimension of a 3-D object. The following terms can all be used to describe the other dimensions of three-dimensional objects: length, width, depth, and breadth. Use these terms and encourage students to use them as well. Emphasize that these terms are used almost interchangeably in everyday language.

Unit 18 **Home Practice**

PART 1

1. $150 - 90 =$ _____
2. $110 - 90 =$ _____
3. $130 - 90 =$ _____
4. $75 +$ _____ $= 120$
5. $500 -$ _____ $= 380$
6. $46 +$ _____ $= 100$

7. Helen's family went canoeing. The canoe's label read: "Maximum load: 350 pounds." Helen's dad weighs 183 pounds. Helen weighs 68 pounds. What's the heaviest a third person can be if he or she rides with Helen and her dad? Show your work.

_____

_____

PART 2

1. $800 + 800 =$ _____
2. $800 + 900 =$ _____
3. $700 + 800 =$ _____
4. $\begin{array}{r} 802 \\ +799 \\ \hline \end{array}$
5. $\begin{array}{r} 815 \\ +885 \\ \hline \end{array}$
6. $\begin{array}{r} 687 \\ +836 \\ \hline \end{array}$

7. Explain a way to solve Question 4 using mental math.

8. Lake Superior, which is the longest Great Lake, is 350 miles long. It is 157 miles longer than Lake Ontario. How long is Lake Ontario?

260 DAB • Grade 3 • Unit 18   VIEWING AND DRAWING 3-D

Discovery Assignment Book - page 260   *(Answers on p. 32)*

Math Facts

DPP items A and B provide practice with the multiplication facts for the square numbers.

Homework and Practice

• Students can collect drawings or pictures of boxes from magazines, newspapers, or store advertisements. Then they can paste these pictures on a sheet of paper, trace the edges of the box shown in the picture, and record the number of faces and edges seen.

• Part 1 of the Home Practice provides practice with addition and subtraction.

• Remind students to practice the multiplication facts for the square numbers using their *Triangle Flash Cards*.

Answers for Part 1 of the Home Practice are in the Answer Key at the end of this lesson and at the end of this unit.

At a Glance

Math Facts and Daily Practice and Problems

DPP items A and B provide practice with the multiplication facts for the square numbers.

Part 1. Three Dimensions

1. Use Mr. Origin and the *Viewing 3-D Objects* Activity Pages in the *Student Guide* to introduce one-, two-, and three-dimensional shapes.
2. Discuss which units can be used to measure length of one-dimensional objects, area of two-dimensional objects, and volume of three-dimensional shapes.

Part 2. Looking at and Describing Boxes

1. Students complete *Questions 4–5* on the *Viewing 3-D Objects* Activity Pages by examining three-dimensional boxes.
2. Students answer *Questions 6–7* by looking at a two-dimensional drawing of a box and comparing it to a real box.

Homework

1. For homework, students collect drawings or pictures of boxes, paste the pictures on paper, trace the edges of each box, and record the number of faces and edges seen.
2. Assign Part 1 of the Home Practice.
3. Students study the multiplication facts for the square numbers using *Triangle Flash Cards*.

Answer Key is on pages 31–32.

Notes:

Triangle Flash Cards: Square Numbers

- Work with a partner. Each partner cuts out the flash cards.

- Your partner chooses one card at a time and covers the shaded number.

- Multiply the two uncovered numbers.

- Divide the used cards into three piles: those you know and can answer quickly, those you can figure out, and those you need to learn.

- Practice the last two piles again. Then make a list of the facts you need to practice at home.

- Repeat the directions for your partner.

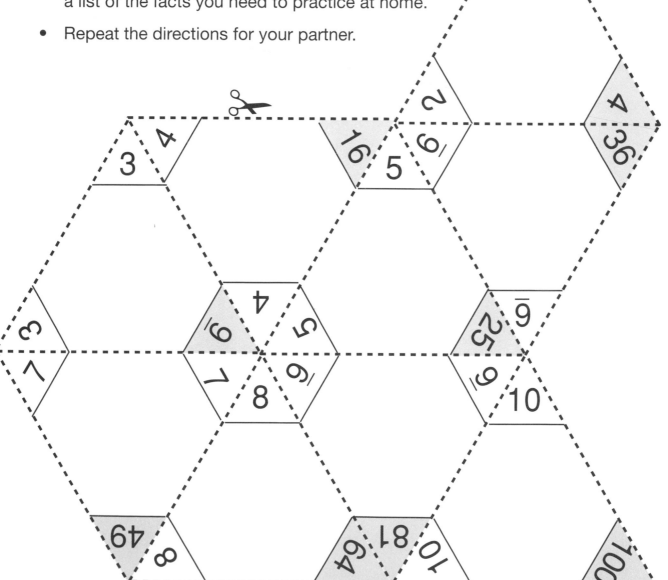

Blackline Master

Student Guide (pp. 266–268)

Viewng 3-D Objects*

1. inches, feet, centimeters, meters, miles

2. square centimeters, square inches, square units

3. cubic centimeters, cubic units

4. **A.** 6 faces

   B. 12 edges

   C. 8 vertices

5. **A.** Put your eyes directly in front of one face of the box.

   B. Looked directly at one edge with the box at eye level.

   C. 3 faces

   D. No, not without changing the box or using a mirror.

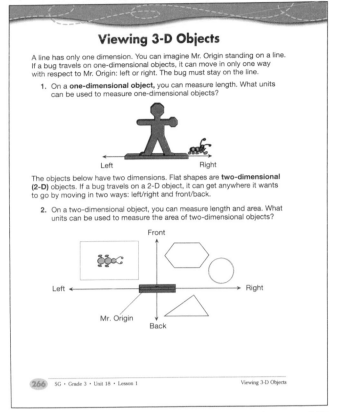

Viewing 3-D Objects

A line has only one dimension. You can imagine Mr. Origin standing on a line. If a bug travels on one-dimensional objects, it can move in only one way with respect to Mr. Origin: left or right. The bug must stay on the line.

1. On a **one-dimensional object,** you can measure length. What units can be used to measure one-dimensional objects?

The objects below have two dimensions. Flat shapes are **two-dimensional (2-D)** objects. If a bug travels on a 2-D object, it can get anywhere it wants to go by moving in two ways: left/right and front/back.

2. On a two-dimensional object, you can measure length and area. What units can be used to measure the area of two-dimensional objects?

266   SG • Grade 3 • Unit 18 • Lesson 1   Viewing 3-D Objects

Student Guide - page 266

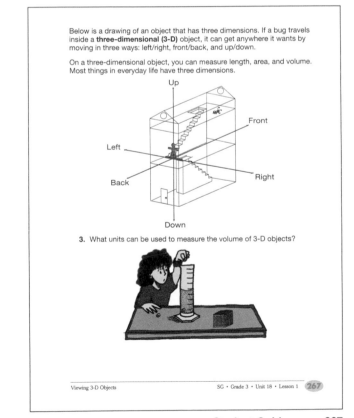

Below is a drawing of an object that has three dimensions. If a bug travels inside a **three-dimensional (3-D)** object, it can get anywhere it wants by moving in three ways: left/right, front/back, and up/down.

On a three-dimensional object, you can measure length, area, and volume. Most things in everyday life have three dimensions.

3. What units can be used to measure the volume of 3-D objects?

Viewing 3-D Objects   SG • Grade 3 • Unit 18 • Lesson 1   267

Student Guide - page 267

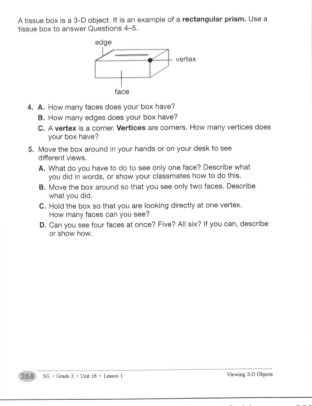

A tissue box is a 3-D object. It is an example of a **rectangular prism.** Use a tissue box to answer Questions 4–5.

4. **A.** How many faces does your box have?

   B. How many edges does your box have?

   C. A **vertex** is a corner. **Vertices** are corners. How many vertices does your box have?

5. Move the box around in your hands or on your desk to see different views.

   A. What do you have to do to see only one face? Describe what you did in words, or show your classmates how to do this.

   B. Move the box around so that you see only two faces. Describe what you did.

   C. Hold the box so that you are looking directly at one vertex. How many faces can you see?

   D. Can you see four faces at once? Five? All six? If you can, describe or show how.

268   SG • Grade 3 • Unit 18 • Lesson 1   Viewing 3-D Objects

Student Guide - page 268

*Answers and/or discussion are included in the Lesson Guide.

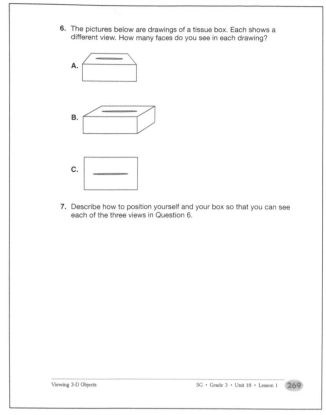

6. The pictures below are drawings of a tissue box. Each shows a different view. How many faces do you see in each drawing?

A.

B.

C.

7. Describe how to position yourself and your box so that you can see each of the three views in Question 6.

Viewing 3-D Objects   SG • Grade 3 • Unit 18 • Lesson 1   269

Student Guide - page 269

Student Guide (p. 269)

6. **A.** 2 faces

 B. 3 faces

 C. 1 face

7. **A.** Look at an edge between the top and a long side.

 B. Look directly at one of the vertices of the top face.

 C. Look from directly above the top face.

Name _____ Date _____

Unit 18 Home Practice

PART 1

1. 150 – 90 = _____
2. 110 – 90 = _____
3. 130 – 90 = _____
4. 75 + _____ = 120
5. 500 – _____ = 380
6. 46 + _____ = 100

7. Helen's family went canoeing. The canoe's label read: "Maximum load: 350 pounds." Helen's dad weighs 183 pounds. Helen weighs 68 pounds. What's the heaviest a third person can be if he or she rides with Helen and her dad? Show your work.

_____

_____

PART 2

1. 800 + 800 = _____
2. 800 + 900 = _____
3. 700 + 800 = _____
4. 802
 +799
5. 815
 +885
6. 687
 +836

7. Explain a way to solve Question 4 using mental math.

8. Lake Superior, which is the longest Great Lake, is 350 miles long. It is 157 miles longer than Lake Ontario. How long is Lake Ontario?

Copyright © Kendall/Hunt Publishing Company

260 DAB • Grade 3 • Unit 18   VIEWING AND DRAWING 3-D

Discovery Assignment Book - page 260

Discovery Assignment Book (p. 260)

Home Practice*

Part 1

1. 60
2. 20
3. 40
4. 45
5. 120
6. 54
7. 99 pounds (350 lbs − 183 lbs = 167 lbs. 167 − 68 lbs = 99 lbs)

*Answers for all the Home Practice in the *Discovery Assignment Book* are at the end of the unit.

Lesson 2

Drawing 3-D Objects

Lesson Overview

Estimated Class Sessions

1

Students compare a two-dimensional drawing of a cube to an actual three-dimensional cube. After comparing and describing faces, edges, angles, and shapes, students draw cubes and other rectangular prisms (boxes).

Key Content

- Translating between a three-dimensional object and a drawing.
- Drawing cubes.
- Drawing rectangular prisms (boxes).

Key Vocabulary

- cube
- parallel
- parallelogram
- quadrilateral
- right angle
- square

Homework

1. Students draw a box at home for homework.
2. Students complete the Journal Prompt at home.
3. Assign Part 2 of the Home Practice.

Assessment

As an assessment, students draw a rectangular prism using a box or other classroom object as a model.

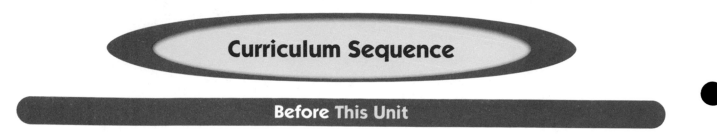

Curriculum Sequence

Before This Unit

Two-Dimensional Shapes

Students investigated two-dimensional shapes in Grade 3 Unit 12 *Dissections*. They counted sides, vertices, and right angles and measured area and perimeter of the shapes.

Materials List

Supplies and Copies

Student	Teacher
Supplies for Each Student • cube (e.g. connecting cube or base-ten piece) • 3 different colored pens or pencils • ruler • masking tape or self-adhesive notes, optional • 12 toothpicks, optional • 8 miniature marshmallows, optional • 3 blue pattern blocks, optional **Supplies for Each Student Pair** • empty cereal box	**Supplies** • 3 overhead blue pattern blocks, optional • large cube (e.g. large base-ten piece or cardboard box) • 12 toothpicks (Extension), optional • 8 miniature marshmallows (Extension), optional
Copies	**Copies/Transparencies**

All blackline masters including assessment, transparency, and DPP masters are also on the Teacher Resource CD.

Student Books
Drawing 3-D Objects (*Student Guide* Pages 270–272)
Working with Cubes (*Discovery Assignment Book* Pages 263–264)
Drawing Rectangular Prisms (*Discovery Assignment Book* Page 265)

Daily Practice and Problems and Home Practice
DPP items C–D (*Unit Resource Guide* Page 16)
Home Practice Part 2 (*Discovery Assignment Book* Page 260)

Note: Classrooms whose pacing differs significantly from the suggested pacing of the units should use the Math Facts Calendar in Section 4 of the *Facts Resource Guide* to ensure students receive the complete math facts program.

Suggestions for using the DPPs are on page 40.

C. Bit: Addition and Subtraction   ⊠ Ⓝ
Practice (URG p. 16)

Complete these problems using pencil and paper or mental math to find the answers.

1. Predict which of the following problems will have the smallest answer (sum or difference).

2.   750   3.   689   4.   148   5.   9145
   − 262   + 851   + 198   − 8997

D. Challenge: Coin Fractions   Ⓝ $
(URG p. 16)

1. Complete the following table:

Name of Coin	Value of Coin (in $)	Fraction of Dollar
penny	$.01	$\frac{1}{100}$
nickel		
dime		
quarter		
half-dollar		
silver dollar		

2. How do you think the quarter and half-dollar got their names?

Before the Activity

Collect empty cereal boxes for students to use as models for drawing rectangular prisms in this activity.

If you plan to do the extension, create an example toothpick-and-marshmallow cube ahead of time by using the instructions in the Extension section of the *Drawing 3-D Objects* Activity Pages in the *Student Guide*.

Teaching the Activity

In Lesson 1 *Viewing 3-D Objects,* students discovered that they can see at most three faces of a box; therefore, any drawing of the outside of a box should show only three faces. In this lesson, they will use this information to draw cubes and other rectangular prisms.

Part 1 | Working with Cubes

The first part of this lesson uses an actual cube and the *Working with Cubes* Activity Pages in the *Discovery Assignment Book.* These pages guide students in an investigation of two-dimensional drawings of cubes.

Before they begin, direct students to examine an actual cube and ask the following:

- *What shape is each face?* (a square)
- *How many faces are there?* (6 faces)
- *How many edges does a cube have?* (12 edges. To keep track of which edges have been counted, students can fold a small piece of tape over each edge and label it with a number.)
- *Hold the cube so that you see three faces by looking at one vertex (corner). What three shapes do you see?*

When students are asked the last question in the set above, many are likely to say, "I see three squares" since they know a cube has square faces. Because the perspective required to see three faces skews each face somewhat, they are actually seeing three parallelograms or other quadrilaterals as shown in Figure 6. Students may have trouble seeing this, so *Questions 1–9* help students use their knowledge of geometry to analyze drawings of cubes. *Question 1* asks students to count the faces they see in the picture of the cube and *Question 2* directs them to trace and count the edges. As students count the edges in the picture, advise them to place a slash mark through each edge as shown so they know the ones they already counted.

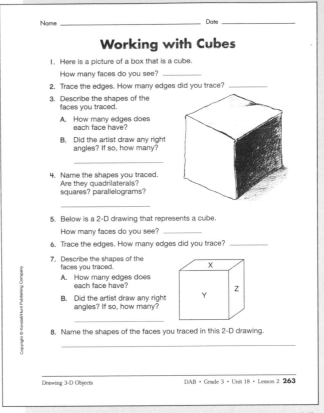

Copyright © Kendall/Hunt Publishing Company

Discovery Assignment Book - page 263 *(Answers on p. 44)*

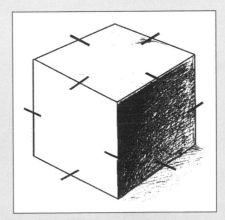

Figure 6: *Cube faces look like parallelograms or other quadrilaterals when viewed from this perspective.*

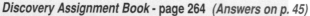
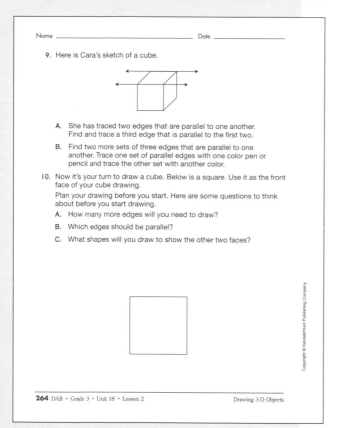

Name _____ Date _____

9. Here is Cara's sketch of a cube.

   A. She has traced two edges that are parallel to one another. Find and trace a third edge that is parallel to the first two.

   B. Find two more sets of three edges that are parallel to one another. Trace one set of parallel edges with one color pen or pencil and trace the other set with another color.

10. Now it's your turn to draw a cube. Below is a square. Use it as the front face of your cube drawing.

   Plan your drawing before you start. Here are some questions to think about before you start drawing.

   A. How many more edges will you need to draw?

   B. Which edges should be parallel?

   C. What shapes will you draw to show the other two faces?

264 DAB • Grade 3 • Unit 18 • Lesson 2   Drawing 3-D Objects

Discovery Assignment Book - page 264 *(Answers on p. 45)*

Question 3 asks students to describe the shapes of the faces they have traced. Each of the three faces has four edges, and none of the angles is a right angle. If students are not convinced, have them use the corner of a sheet of paper to test the corners of the faces to see that they are not right angles. Students name these shapes in *Question 4.* Make sure students are familiar with the terms. See the Content Note. Since each face has four sides, they are all quadrilaterals. They also appear to be parallelograms, but a more rigorous inspection shows that all the pairs of sides may not really be parallel. Whether they are parallelograms or just quadrilaterals need not be discussed at great length. It is important, however, to note that none of the shapes traced on this drawing has right angles; therefore, they are not squares.

When an artist sketches a cube, it is customary to draw the front face as a square with the other two faces drawn as parallelograms. *Questions 5–8* analyze this type of sketch. *Question 9* asks students to identify the parallel edges in such a drawing. They can identify three sets of parallel lines using different colored pens or pencils to trace each set. Figure 7 shows parallel edges of a cube drawing.

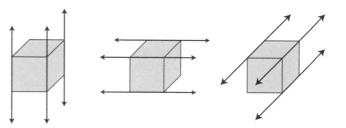

Figure 7: *Three sets of parallel edges shown on a drawing of a cube*

Question 10 asks students to draw their own cube by adding on to the front square provided. Have students share their work. They can discuss their drawings using prompts similar to *Questions 1–10.*

Part 2 Drawing 3-D Objects

The second part of this lesson is found on the *Drawing 3-D Objects* Activity Pages in the *Student Guide.* *Question 1* presents students with two inaccurate drawings and one accurate depiction of a cube. By using the information from the *Working with Cubes* Activity Pages in the *Discovery Assignment Book* and by looking carefully at an actual cube, students should

Drawing 3-D Objects

Drawing a Cube by Showing Three Faces

You can use geometry to help you learn to draw a cube. Studying the edges, faces, and vertices of a cube will help you draw what you see when you look at a cube. A **cube** is a box that has six faces. All the edges of a cube are the same length.

1. Here are 3 sketches of a cube. Which look like a cube? Which do not? Explain your choices.

   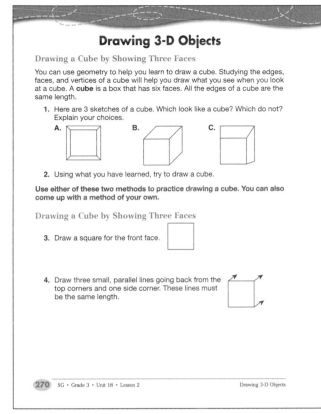

   A.   B.   C.

2. Using what you have learned, try to draw a cube.

Use either of these two methods to practice drawing a cube. You can also come up with a method of your own.

Drawing a Cube by Showing Three Faces

3. Draw a square for the front face.

4. Draw three small, parallel lines going back from the top corners and one side corner. These lines must be the same length.

Student Guide - page 270 *(Answers on p. 43)*

---

5. Draw two connecting lines. The first line should be along the top, and the second line should be along the side.

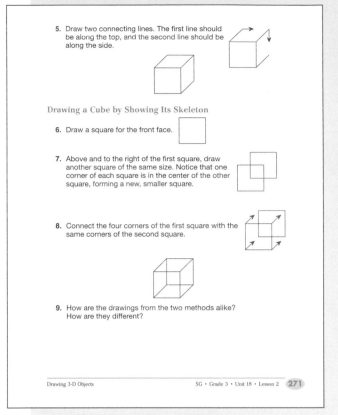

Drawing a Cube by Showing Its Skeleton

6. Draw a square for the front face.

7. Above and to the right of the first square, draw another square of the same size. Notice that one corner of each square is in the center of the other square, forming a new, smaller square.

8. Connect the four corners of the first square with the same corners of the second square.

9. How are the drawings from the two methods alike? How are they different?

Student Guide - page 271 *(Answers on p. 43)*

---

be able to identify the second drawing (B) as correct and identify the mistakes in the other two drawings. Include the following terms in discussing the sketches: shapes, faces, edges, angles, and parallel lines. The first drawing (A) shows too many faces and edges. The appropriate edges in the third drawing (C) are not parallel to one another. *Question 2* asks students to try drawing a cube based on their work so far.

The drawings students make for *Question 2* can be used for comparison with the ones students will make by following the directions in the next section. This section describes two possible methods for sketching a cube. Students should not be confined to using only these two methods. Encourage them to use and to share their own methods as well.

In the Extension section, students are shown how to use toothpicks and marshmallows to build a 3-D model of a cube. You may wish to create this 3-D model of a cube ahead of time so that students can compare it to the sketch during this activity.

Extension

You can use toothpicks and small marshmallows to make a 3-D cube model of your own. You will need one toothpick for each cube edge. You will also need 8 marshmallows for the vertices, which you can use to connect the toothpicks.

A. Stick one end of a toothpick into a marshmallow.

B. Make a square corner by sticking another toothpick into the marshmallow.

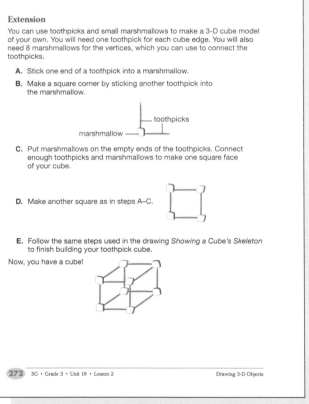

C. Put marshmallows on the empty ends of the toothpicks. Connect enough toothpicks and marshmallows to make one square face of your cube.

D. Make another square as in steps A–C.

E. Follow the same steps used in the drawing *Showing a Cube's Skeleton* to finish building your toothpick cube.

Now, you have a cube!

Student Guide - page 272

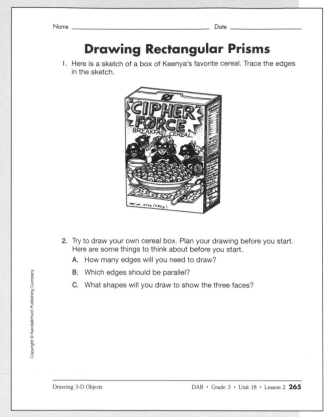

Name _____ Date _____

Drawing Rectangular Prisms

1. Here is a sketch of a box of Keenya's favorite cereal. Trace the edges in the sketch.

2. Try to draw your own cereal box. Plan your drawing before you start. Here are some things to think about before you start.
   A. How many edges will you need to draw?
   B. Which edges should be parallel?
   C. What shapes will you draw to show the three faces?

Drawing 3-D Objects   DAB • Grade 3 • Unit 18 • Lesson 2 **265**

Discovery Assignment Book - page 265 (Answers on p. 45)

Name _____ Date _____

Unit 18 Home Practice

PART 1
1. 150 – 90 = _____
2. 110 – 90 = _____
3. 130 – 90 = _____
4. 75 + _____ = 120
5. 500 – _____ = 380
6. 46 + _____ = 100

7. Helen's family went canoeing. The canoe's label read: "Maximum load: 350 pounds." Helen's dad weighs 183 pounds. Helen weighs 68 pounds. What's the heaviest a third person can be if he or she rides with Helen and her dad? Show your work.

_____
_____

PART 2
1. 800 + 800 = _____
2. 800 + 900 = _____
3. 700 + 800 = _____
4. 802
   +799
5. 815
   +885
6. 687
   +836

7. Explain a way to solve Question 4 using mental math.

8. Lake Superior, which is the longest Great Lake, is 350 miles long. It is 157 miles longer than Lake Ontario. How long is Lake Ontario?

260 DAB • Grade 3 • Unit 18   VIEWING AND DRAWING 3-D

Discovery Assignment Book - page 260 (Answers on p. 44)

Part 3 Drawing Rectangular Prisms

The *Drawing Rectangular Prisms* Activity Page in the *Discovery Assignment Book* extends students' work with cubes to other rectangular prisms such as cereal boxes. After tracing an example picture of a cereal box, students are asked to sketch their own cereal box. Before students attempt to draw the box, discuss the differences between a sketch of a cube and a sketch of the cereal box using the prompts on the page. Students will find actual empty cereal boxes a helpful reference in making and checking their drawings.

Journal Prompt

What does learning to draw a cube have to do with mathematics?

Homework and Practice

- During class, discuss different boxes students may have in their homes. Then ask students to make a sketch of a box they have at home and bring their work to school.

- Assign the Journal Prompt for homework. You can use this prompt to strengthen students' understanding of the nature of mathematics as well as assess their attitudes toward math. Mathematics is more than memorizing facts and practicing algorithms. The visualizing, describing, and recording of three-dimensional objects in this unit show students how we can look at everyday objects mathematically. In this activity, students use geometric terms such as vertex, edge, face, parallelogram, and quadrilateral and geometric concepts to analyze drawings of cubes.

- DPP Bit C provides practice with addition and subtraction using pencil and paper or mental math. For Challenge D, students name the value of coins and identify what fraction of a dollar they are.

- You may assign Part 2 of the Home Practice for homework. It provides computation practice.

Answers for Part 2 of the Home Practice are in the Answer Key at the end of this lesson and at the end of this unit.

Have students form groups and give each group a box (a rectangular prism other than a cereal box). Ask each student to draw the box. Students label their drawings and write descriptions of the characteristics that helped them make them. Some suitable large rectangular prisms include a filing cabinet, a box from an order of books, and a pizza delivery box. Smaller boxes from a number of household items include those from frozen dinners, spaghetti, cookies, laundry detergent, and plastic drinking straws.

Extension

- Students build a cube from toothpicks and marshmallows as described in the *Student Guide*. Each student will need 12 toothpicks and 8 marshmallows.

- Have students draw the cereal box again, but this time from a different viewpoint. For example, draw the box as it would look if they were reading the side containing the nutritional information or as it would look lying on its side.

- Before or during class, take photographs of different views of boxes with an instant camera. Trace along the edges of the boxes in the photographs and discuss the shapes of the faces, the number of faces, the number of edges, and parallel lines.

- Have students draw a cube by tracing three blue pattern block pieces as shown in Figure 8. Remind students that although these three faces are drawn as parallelograms, they are actually squares on the real object. Point out that a cube cannot be drawn in the correct perspective using the square pattern block pieces.

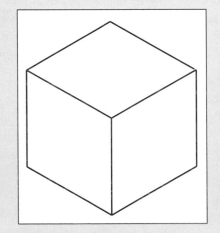

Figure 8: *A cube made from three blue pattern block pieces*

At a Glance

Math Facts and Daily Practice and Problems

DPP Bit C provides practice with computation and mental math. Challenge D involves money and fractions.

Part 1. Working with Cubes

1. Students examine an actual cube by counting faces and edges.
2. They view the cube so they can see three faces and describe the shapes they see.
3. Students analyze 2-D drawings of cubes using the *Working with Cubes* Activity Pages in the *Discovery Assignment Book.*
4. Students trace a drawing of a cube and analyze the shapes they drew.
5. Students draw a cube.

Part 2. Drawing 3-D Objects

1. Students analyze inaccurate drawings of cubes on the *Drawing 3-D Objects* Activity Pages in the *Student Guide.*
2. Students practice drawing cubes using directions given in the *Drawing 3-D Objects* Activity Pages.

Part 3. Drawing Rectangular Prisms

1. Students analyze drawings of rectangular prisms (boxes) using the *Drawing Rectangular Prisms* Activity Page in the *Discovery Assignment Book.*
2. Students make drawings of rectangular prisms using cereal boxes as models.

Homework

1. Students draw a box at home for homework.
2. Students complete the Journal Prompt at home.
3. Assign Part 2 of the Home Practice.

Assessment

As an assessment, students draw a rectangular prism using a box or other classroom object as a model.

Extension

1. Have students build a cube from toothpicks and marshmallows.
2. Have students draw the cereal box from different viewpoints.
3. Take photographs of different views of boxes. Discuss shapes of faces and number of faces, edges, and parallel lines.
4. Have students draw a cube by tracing three blue pattern block pieces. Point out that a cube cannot be drawn in the correct perspective using square pattern block pieces.

Answer Key is on pages 43–45.

Notes:

Student Guide (p. 270)

Drawing 3-D Objects*

1. **A.** It does not look like a cube. When looking at a cube you can only see three sides at one time unless you disassemble it or use a mirror.

   B. It looks like a cube. The three faces are parallelograms; the front face is a square.

   C. It does not look like a cube. The appropriate edges of the faces are not parallel.

2. Compare students' sketches of a cube to figure B in *Question 1.*

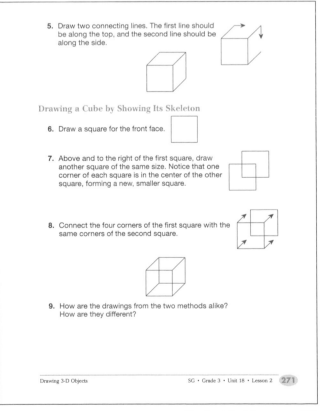

Student Guide - page 270

Student Guide (p. 271)

9. Answers will vary. Some possible responses:

   Alike—same shape (cube), opposite edges are parallel, front face is a square.

   Different—can see all edges, vertices, and faces in the skeleton type of cube.

Student Guide - page 271

*Answers and/or discussion are included in the Lesson Guide.

Name _____ Date _____

Unit 18 Home Practice

PART 1

1. 150 − 90 = _____
2. 110 − 90 = _____
3. 130 − 90 = _____
4. 75 + _____ = 120
5. 500 − _____ = 380
6. 46 + _____ = 100

7. Helen's family went canoeing. The canoe's label read: "Maximum load: 350 pounds." Helen's dad weighs 183 pounds. Helen weighs 68 pounds. What's the heaviest a third person can be if he or she rides with Helen and her dad? Show your work.

_____

_____

PART 2

1. 800 + 800 = _____
2. 800 + 900 = _____
3. 700 + 800 = _____
4. 802
   +799
5. 815
   +885
6. 687
   +836

7. Explain a way to solve Question 4 using mental math.

8. Lake Superior, which is the longest Great Lake, is 350 miles long. It is 157 miles longer than Lake Ontario. How long is Lake Ontario?

260 DAB • Grade 3 • Unit 18   VIEWING AND DRAWING 3-D

Discovery Assignment Book - page 260

Discovery Assignment Book (p. 260)

Home Practice*

Part 2

1. 1600
2. 1700
3. 1500
4. 1601
5. 1700
6. 1523
7. Possible strategy: $800 + 2 + 700 + 99$
   $= 800 + 700 + 101 = 1601$
8. 193 miles

Name _____ Date _____

Working with Cubes

1. Here is a picture of a box that is a cube.
   How many faces do you see? _____
2. Trace the edges. How many edges did you trace? _____
3. Describe the shapes of the faces you traced.
   A. How many edges does each face have?
   B. Did the artist draw any right angles? If so, how many?

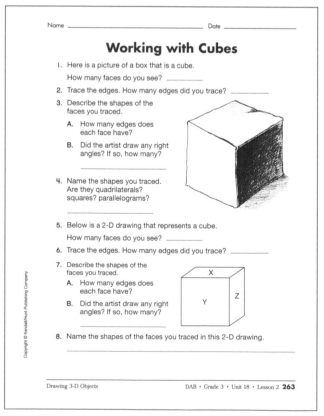

4. Name the shapes you traced. Are they quadrilaterals? squares? parallelograms?
   _____

5. Below is a 2-D drawing that represents a cube.
   How many faces do you see? _____
6. Trace the edges. How many edges did you trace? _____
7. Describe the shapes of the faces you traced.
   A. How many edges does each face have?
   B. Did the artist draw any right angles? If so, how many?

8. Name the shapes of the faces you traced in this 2-D drawing.
   _____

Drawing 3-D Objects   DAB • Grade 3 • Unit 18 • Lesson 2 **263**

Discovery Assignment Book - page 263

Discovery Assignment Book (p. 263)

Working with Cubes†

1. 3 faces
2. 9 edges
3. **A.** All three faces have 4 edges.
   B. None of the three shapes in the drawing have right angles.
4. quadrilaterals; shapes may appear to be parallelograms but you can only be sure that these shapes are quadrilaterals
5. 3 faces
6. 9 edges
7. **A.** 4 edges
   B. Face Y has 4 right angles. The other faces do not have a right angle.
8. Shapes X, Y, and Z are all parallelograms. Shape Y is also a square.

---

*Answers for all the Home Practice in the *Discovery Assignment Book* are at the end of the unit.
†Answers and/or discussion are included in the Lesson Guide.

Discovery Assignment Book (p. 264)

9. **A.**

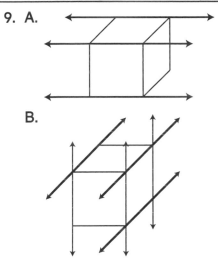

B.

10. **A.** 5 edges

B. One edge will be parallel to the top and bottom edges of the square. One edge will be parallel to the vertical sides of the square. Three new edges will be drawn parallel to one another.

C. parallelograms

Discovery Assignment Book (p. 265)

Drawing Rectangular Prisms*

1. 9 edges should be traced.

2. **A.** 9 edges

B. There should be three sets of parallel lines.

C. Answers will vary. One rectangle and two parallelograms, or three parallelograms, or three kinds of quadrilaterals.

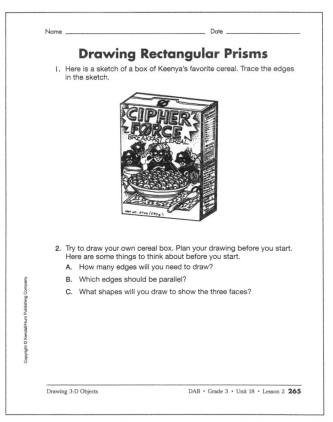

Discovery Assignment Book - page 264

Discovery Assignment Book - page 265

*Answers and/or discussion are included in the Lesson Guide.

Lesson 3

Building and Planning Cube Models

Lesson Overview

Students build cube models using two-dimensional representations called cube model plans to describe them. Students use cube model plans to determine the area of a cube model's base, its volume, and its height. Students also build cube models according to specifications on cube model plans and, in the process, solve problems with multiple solutions.

Key Content

- Building a cube model using a cube model plan.
- Drawing cube model plans to describe a cube model.
- Finding the area of a cube model's base, its volume, and its height.
- Solving problems with multiple solutions.

Key Vocabulary

- base
- cube model plan
- cubic units
- floor plan
- square units
- units

Math Facts

DPP Bit E provides practice with multiplication facts for the square numbers.

Homework

Assign Part 3 of the Home Practice.

Assessment

Use the *Observational Assessment Record* to record students' abilities to translate between a cube model, its cube model plan, and a drawing.

Curriculum Sequence

Before This Unit

Students have had experience with cube models in both first and second grades. In Grade 1 Unit 12 *Cubes and Volume* they found the volume of simple cube models by counting the number of cubes. In Grade 2 Unit 7 *Building with Cubes* they translated between a cube model and its cube model plan and used different strategies, including counting cubes and writing number sentences, to find volume.

After This Unit

Students will build on their exploration of three-dimensional objects in Grade 4 Unit 9 *Shapes and Solids*.

Materials List

Supplies and Copies

Student	Teacher
Supplies for Each Student Pair • 30 connecting cubes	**Supplies**
Copies • 3 copies of *3 × 3 Cube Model Plans* per student (*Unit Resource Guide* Page 55)	**Copies/Transparencies** • 1 transparency of *3 × 3 Cube Model Plans*, optional (*Unit Resource Guide* Page 55) • 1 transparency of *Dee's Cube Model Plan* (*Unit Resource Guide* Page 56) • 1 copy of *Observational Assessment Record* to be used throughout this unit (*Unit Resource Guide* Pages 11–12)

All blackline masters including assessment, transparency, and DPP masters are also on the Teacher Resource CD.

Student Books

Building and Planning Cube Models (*Student Guide* Pages 273–276)

Daily Practice and Problems

DPP items E–F (*Unit Resource Guide* Page 17)
Home Practice Part 3 (*Discovery Assignment Book* Page 261)

Note: Classrooms whose pacing differs significantly from the suggested pacing of the units should use the Math Facts Calendar in Section 4 of the *Facts Resource Guide* to ensure students receive the complete math facts program.

Assessment Tools

Observational Assessment Record (*Unit Resource Guide* Pages 11–12)

E. Bit: Story Solving (URG p. 17)

$\begin{array}{r} 5 \\ \times\,7 \\ \hline \end{array}$

Write a story and draw a picture about 8×8. Write a number sentence for your picture.

F. Challenge: Containers (URG p. 17)   [N] [⚖]

Suppose you have one empty container that holds exactly 5 quarts and another empty container that holds exactly 2 quarts. Figure out a way to measure exactly 1 quart of water by pouring water between the containers. You can use as much water from the faucet as you wish.

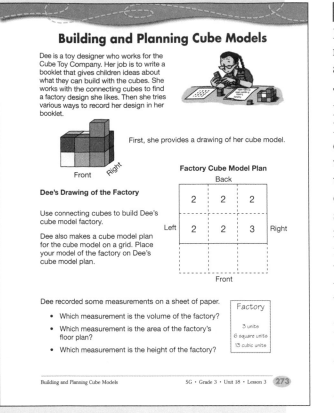

Building and Planning Cube Models

Dee is a toy designer who works for the Cube Toy Company. Her job is to write a booklet that gives children ideas about what they can build with the cubes. She works with the connecting cubes to find a factory design she likes. Then she tries various ways to record her design in her booklet.

First, she provides a drawing of her cube model.

Front   Right

Dee's Drawing of the Factory

Use connecting cubes to build Dee's cube model factory.

Dee also makes a cube model plan for the cube model on a grid. Place your model of the factory on Dee's cube model plan.

Factory Cube Model Plan

Back

	2	2	2	
Left	2	2	3	Right

Front

Dee recorded some measurements on a sheet of paper.

- Which measurement is the volume of the factory?
- Which measurement is the area of the factory's floor plan?
- Which measurement is the height of the factory?

Factory
3 units
6 square units
13 cubic units

Student Guide - page 273

Turn your factory upside down. What shape is the floor of the factory?

The bottom of a model is called its **base**, or **floor plan.** The base is outlined on the cube model plan. Place the bottom of your factory directly on top of the cube model plan again. Be sure the front of the factory is toward the front of the plan.

Dee looked at the building from above to draw the cube model plan. Now place your factory beside the cube model plan. Look at the numbers written on the plan. What do you think the numbers stand for?

A cube model plan provides lots of information about a cube model. You can find the area of a cube model's base, its volume, and its height.

Dee uses rules in making her cube models. Dee's cube model plans only work if we stack cubes in a certain way.

These pictures represent some rules for making cube models. Can you explain them in words? Why do you think we use these rules?

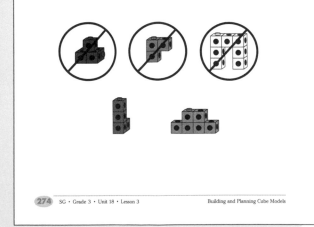

Student Guide - page 274

In this activity, students create and record cube model plans for constructions. They also tell height, area of base, and volume from cube model plans.

The *Building and Planning Cube Models* Activity Pages in the *Student Guide* introduce students to Dee, a toy designer. Dee has made a cube model called "factory." She recorded her factory model as a two-dimensional drawing. Read through the directions on the page with students. Instruct them to use connecting cubes to build a model of the factory as shown in the drawing. Dee also records her factory model as a cube model plan. Students compare the factory they built to Dee's cube model plan shown in the *Student Guide*. This plan is like a blueprint. It tells the height, volume, and area of the factory's base.

Dee has written several measurements describing the factory on a piece of paper. Students are asked to figure out what each measurement represents. The units give students the clues they need to answer the questions. For example, since cubic units are used to measure volume, 13 cubic units is the volume of the factory. Students should also be able to see that their model is made with 13 cubes. The six square units describe the area of the base. The measurement for the height is 3 units. Note that 3 units is also the measurement for the width of the model. Remind students to use proper units when measuring length, area, and volume. In this activity and the next, we simply use **unit, square unit,** and **cubic unit,** respectively.

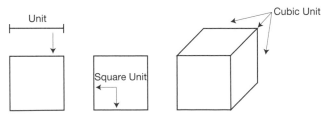

Figure 9: *Units for length, area, and volume of connecting cubes*

After students find the measurements, they flip over their model and describe the shape of the floor. Have students compare their cube models of the factory to Dee's cube model plan. To do this, have students place their factory models on their desks with the front towards them and look at the top of the models from directly above. Guide students to the realization that each cube looks like a square from this bird's-eye view. Then, show the *Dee's Cube Model Plan*

Transparency Master on the overhead projector as you tell the following story.

> *Dee looks down on the factory model from overhead. She makes a map of the factory and calls this map a cube model plan. On it she records the number of cubes used in each column of the six-column factory. Notice that one column is three cubes high while each of the other columns is two cubes high.*

Students are asked to place the factory on the cube model plan on the *Building and Planning Cube Models* Activity Pages again. (All cube model plans are drawn on dotted line grids.) Do the same on the overhead. Demonstrate how the rectangular base was drawn on the cube model plan by tracing the bottom of the factory model directly on the transparency grid. Emphasize that the terms **floor plan** and **base** both describe the shape of the bottom of a cube model. In this case, the base's shape is a 2-by-3 rectangle and its area is 6 square units.

Tell students to look at their cube model plans. Ask:

- *What is the height of the factory?* (3 units)

Have them explain how they can use the cube model plan to find the height. Make sure students realize that the height refers to the tallest column. Help students understand why the measurement is made in this way by relating it to their own heights. Ask students if their heights are measured to their shoulders or to the top of their heads. Measuring to the highest point is a common way to measure height. The height of the tallest column in the factory is 3 units.

Ask,

- *How do you know the volume of the factory?* (By counting the cubes, 13 cubic units)

Some students will count the cubes in their models while others will look at the cube model plan. Still others will refer to the piece of paper on Dee's desk. Direct their attention to the cube model plan. Then ask,

- *If all you had was the cube model plan, how would you know the volume?* (The sum of the numbers in the cube model plan represents the volume of the cube model.)

After students compare the factory and its cube model plan, they are ready to learn the rules they need to follow when using cube model plans. The artwork on the *Building and Planning Cube Models* Activity Pages shows some rules that must be

Content Note

Units. The connecting cubes used in this activity and the following activity have edges that measure two centimeters. Therefore, the area of one face is four square centimeters and the volume of one cube is 2 cm $\times$ 2 cm $\times$ 2 cm or eight cubic centimeters. To simplify the activity, we define one unit to be the length of one edge of a connecting cube. The area of one face is one square unit while the volume of one cube is one cubic unit.

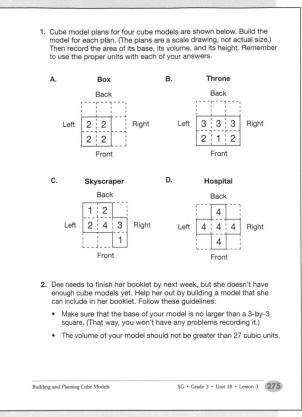

1. Cube model plans for four cube models are shown below. Build the model for each plan. (The plans are a scale drawing, not actual size.) Then record the area of its base, its volume, and its height. Remember to use the proper units with each of your answers.

A.   **Box**
              Back
       ┌───┬───┐
Left │ 2 │ 2 │ Right
       ├───┼───┤
       │ 2 │ 2 │
       └───┴───┘
             Front

B.   **Throne**
              Back
       ┌───┬───┬───┐
Left │ 3 │ 3 │ 3 │ Right
       ├───┼───┼───┤
       │ 2 │ 1 │ 2 │
       └───┴───┴───┘
               Front

C.   **Skyscraper**
              Back
       ┌───┬───┐
       │ 1 │ 2 │
       ├───┼───┼───┐
Left │ 2 │ 4 │ 3 │ Right
       └───┼───┼───┘
           │ 1 │
           └───┘
             Front

D.   **Hospital**
              Back
           ┌───┐
           │ 4 │
       ┌───┼───┼───┐
Left │ 4 │ 4 │ 4 │ Right
       └───┼───┼───┘
           │ 4 │
           └───┘
             Front

2. Dee needs to finish her booklet by next week, but she doesn't have enough cube models yet. Help her out by building a model that she can include in her booklet. Follow these guidelines:

   • Make sure that the base of your model is no larger than a 3-by-3 square. (That way, you won't have any problems recording it.)

   • The volume of your model should not be greater than 27 cubic units.

Student Guide - page 275 (Answers on p. 57)

• Record your cube model in a cube model plan. You can use a copy of the *3 × 3 Cube Model Plans* Activity Page.

• Give a name to the model you create. Write the name on the plan.

3. Build the models described in A through F. Then make a cube model plan for each. (Hint: There may be more than one answer; sometimes, no solution is possible.)

   A. The floor plan is a 2-by-3 rectangle. The height is 3 units. The volume is 17 cubic units.

   B. The base has an area of 6 square units. The floor plan is not a rectangle. The volume is 24 cubic units.

   C. The floor plan is a 3-by-3 square. The height is 3 units. The volume is 26 cubic units.

   D. The volume is 18 cubic units. The floor plan is a 3-by-3 square. The height is 2 units.

   E. The area of the base is 4 square units. The height is 3 units. The volume is 14 cubic units.

   F. The volume is 30 cubic units. The height is 5 units.

Student Guide - page 276 (Answers on pp. 57–58)

---

followed in building cube models so they can be recorded on cube model plans. You can explain the building restrictions:

1. Cubes must always be attached face to face. This rule ensures that the model can be described in terms of columns. The height of each column is recorded on the cube model plan.

2. No balconies (overhangs) or arches are allowed. This rule ensures that each cube model plan describes one and only one cube model. Thus, when the number 1 is recorded in a square of a cube model plan, we know that the one cube in that column is on the base, not above it.

In **Question 1,** students are asked to build four cube models from four different cube model plans. Review how to use cube model plans on a grid using the bottom half of the *Dee's Cube Model Plan* Transparency Master. A student or group of students can design and build a cube model, show it on the overhead, and then create a cube model plan. For each model, students find the area of its base, its volume, and its height, using both the model they built and the cube model plan. Help students visualize the cube columns that make up each model. For instance, the model in **Question 1A** has four columns of two cubes each.

Show how the models in **Question 1** follow the rules for building cube model plans. Demonstrate that the model in **Question 1C** could represent a number of different buildings if we allowed balconies or arches.

In **Question 2,** students are asked to build a model for Dee. This exercise will help you assess whether students understand the rules for building cube models and whether they can record their model on a cube model plan, using a copy of *3 × 3 Cube Model Plans* Blackline Master. Since the page consists of individual 3-by-3 grids, students are restricted to a floor plan no larger than a 3-by-3 square. They also are limited to 27 cubes in their buildings. You may wish to discuss floor plans they may or may not use. For example, they cannot choose a 2-by-4 floor plan. However, they can have a floor plan with an area of 8 square units by choosing other layouts.

In **Question 3,** students must build six cube models according to written specifications. Have students work in pairs. Once a pair builds each model, they record the answer on a copy of the *3 × 3 Cube Model Plans* Blackline Master. Except for Model E, all the models have one or more possible solutions. (Model D has only one solution and Model E has no possible solution.) Ask students to share their answers.

Math Facts

DPP Bit E provides practice with the multiplication facts for the square numbers.

Homework and Practice

- For DPP Challenge F students use their knowledge of volume to solve a problem.

- Part 3 of the Home Practice expands on the activity of the lesson with cube models and cube model plans.

- Remind students to continue practicing the multiplication facts for the square numbers using the *Triangle Flash Cards*.

Answers for Part 3 of the Home Practice are in the Answer Key at the end of this lesson and at the end of this unit.

Assessment

Use the *Observational Assessment Record* to document students' abilities to translate between a cube model and its cube model plan, and a drawing.

Extension

- Students build three or four cube models and record a cube model plan for each. Then they exchange plans and build each other's cube models. Students will need additional copies of the *3 × 3 Cube Model Plans* Activity Page.

- Students use copies of *Centimeter Grid Paper* instead of the *3 × 3 Cube Model Plans* Activity Page so they can build and record cube models with larger bases.

- Students devise a new way of making a cube model plan for simple cube models that have balconies or arches.

Name _____ Date _____

PART 3

1. What units can be used to measure:
   A. the length of your finger? _____
   B. the area of your hand? _____
   C. the volume of a cereal box? _____

2. What is the volume of the cube model which is built using this plan?

   _____

4	3	4
2	1	4

3. Make a different cube model plan on a sheet of paper. Keep the volume the same as in Question 2. You may change the floor plan.

PART 4

1. Skip count by fives backwards from 80. Record the numbers below as you say them.

   _____
   _____

2. Skip count by fours backwards from 60. Record the numbers.

   _____
   _____

3. 6 × 3 = _____   4. 6 × 30 = _____   5. 6 × 300 = _____

6. Explain how you would find the answer to 6 × 29. _____

   _____
   _____

VIEWING AND DRAWING 3-D   DAB • Grade 3 • Unit 18 **261**

Discovery Assignment Book - page 261 (Answers on p. 58)

At a Glance

Math Facts and Daily Practice and Problems

DPP Bit E provides practice with multiplication facts for the square numbers. Challenge F is an open-ended problem.

Teaching the Activity

1. Students read the *Building and Planning Cube Models* Activity Pages in the *Student Guide*.
2. Students build a cube model factory and compare it to a cube model plan.
3. Students identify the measurement for the volume, area of the base, and the height of the cube model.
4. Use the *Dee's Cube Model Plan* Transparency Master to compare cube models to cube model plans.
5. Students learn the rules for building cube models.
6. In *Question 1,* students build cube models from cube model plans and tell the volume, area of base, and height of cube models.
7. In *Question 2,* students design and build cube models and record them on cube model plans.
8. In *Question 3,* students build cube models from information given.

Homework

Assign Part 3 of the Home Practice.

Assessment

Use the *Observational Assessment Record* to record students' abilities to translate between a cube model, its cube model plan, and a drawing.

Extension

1. Have students build 3 or 4 cube models, record the plans, and exchange the plans with a partner.
2. Have students use *Centimeter Grid Paper* to make plans for larger cube models.
3. Have students devise a plan for models with balconies or arches.

Answer Key is on pages 57–58.

Notes:

Name _____   Date _____

3 × 3 Cube Model Plans

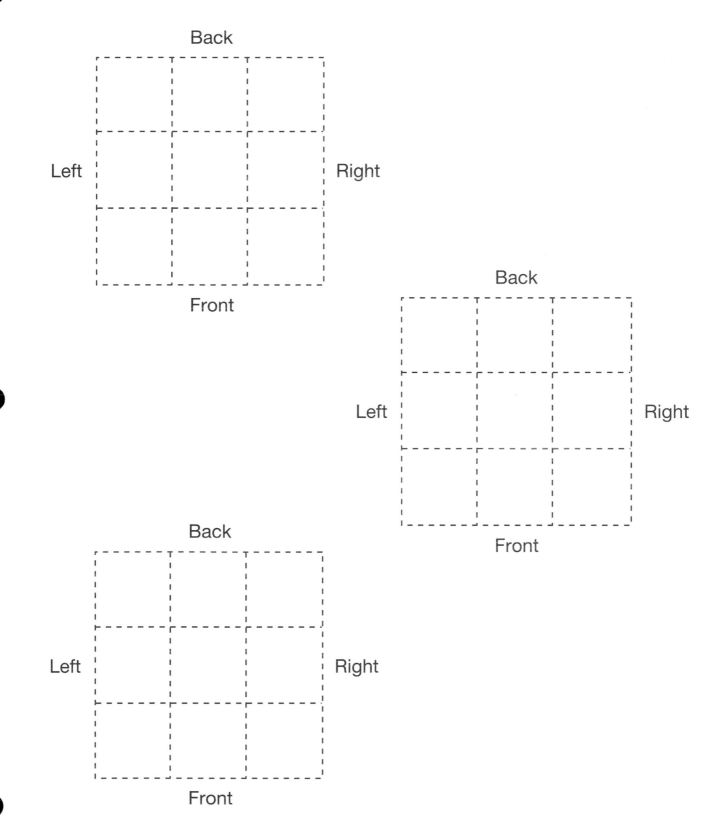

Dee's Cube Model Plan

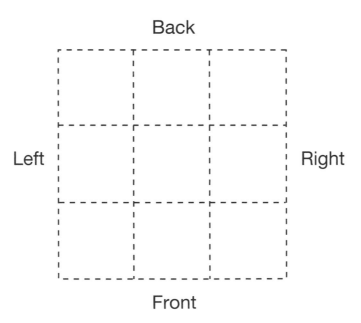

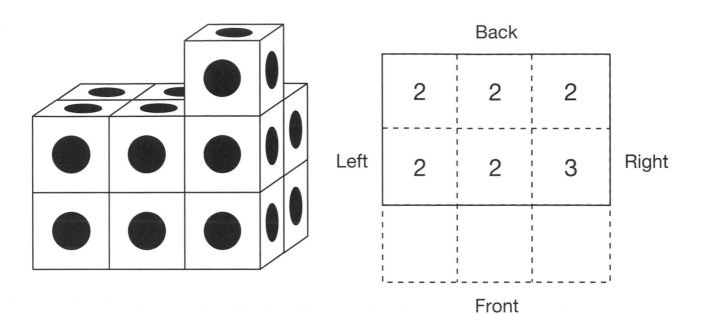

Height = 3 units
Volume = 13 cubic units
Area of Base = 6 square units

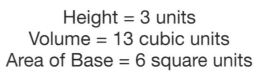

Transparency Master

Student Guide (pp. 275–276)

Building and Planning Cube Models*

I. A. Area = 4 sq units

Height = 2 units

Volume = 8 cubic units

B. Area = 6 sq units

Height = 3 units

Volume = 14 cubic units

C. Area = 6 sq units

Height = 4 units

Volume = 13 cubic units

D. Area = 5 sq units

Height = 4 units

Volume = 20 cubic units

2. Answers will vary.

3. A. Answers will vary. Here is one example.

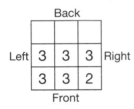

B. Answers will vary. Here is one example.

C. Answers will vary. Here is one example.

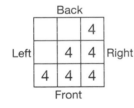

D.

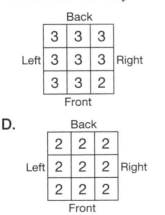

E. There is no solution. With a base area of 4 square units and a height of 3 units, the largest possible volume is 12 cubic units.

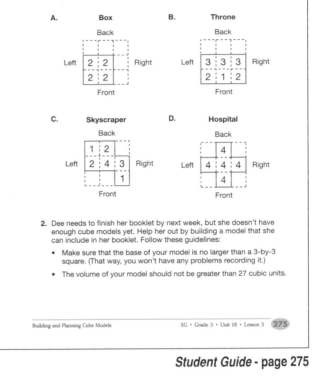

1. Cube model plans for four cube models are shown below. Build the model for each plan. (The plans are a scale drawing, not actual size.) Then record the area of its base, its volume, and its height. Remember to use the proper units with each of your answers.

A. **Box**
B. **Throne**
C. **Skyscraper**
D. **Hospital**

2. Dee needs to finish her booklet by next week, but she doesn't have enough cube models yet. Help her out by building a model that she can include in her booklet. Follow these guidelines:

- Make sure that the base of your model is no larger than a 3-by-3 square. (That way, you won't have any problems recording it.)
- The volume of your model should not be greater than 27 cubic units.

Building and Planning Cube Models   SG • Grade 3 • Unit 18 • Lesson 3   275

Student Guide - page 275

- Record your cube model in a cube model plan. You can use a copy of the 3 × 3 *Cube Model Plans* Activity Page.
- Give a name to the model you create. Write the name on the plan.

3. Build the models described in A through F. Then make a cube model plan for each. (Hint: There may be more than one answer; sometimes, no solution is possible.)

A. The floor plan is a 2-by-3 rectangle. The height is 3 units. The volume is 17 cubic units.

B. The base has an area of 6 square units. The floor plan is not a rectangle. The volume is 24 cubic units.

C. The floor plan is a 3-by-3 square. The height is 3 units. The volume is 26 cubic units.

D. The volume is 18 cubic units. The floor plan is a 3-by-3 square. The height is 2 units.

E. The area of the base is 4 square units. The height is 3 units. The volume is 14 cubic units.

F. The volume is 30 cubic units. The height is 5 units.

276   SG • Grade 3 • Unit 18 • Lesson 3   Building and Planning Cube Models

Student Guide - page 276

*Answers and/or discussion are included in the Lesson Guide.

F. Answers will vary. Here is one example.

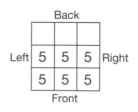

Back

| Left | 5 | 5 | 5 | Right |

Front

Name _____ Date _____

PART 3

1. What units can be used to measure:
   A. the length of your finger? _____
   B. the area of your hand? _____
   C. the volume of a cereal box? _____

2. What is the volume of the cube model which is built using this plan?

   _____

   | 4 | 3 | 4 |
   | 2 | 1 | 4 |

3. Make a different cube model plan on a sheet of paper. Keep the volume the same as in Question 2. You may change the floor plan.

PART 4

1. Skip count by fives backwards from 80. Record the numbers below as you say them.

   _____
   _____

2. Skip count by fours backwards from 60. Record the numbers.

   _____
   _____

3. 6 × 3 = _____   4. 6 × 30 = _____   5. 6 × 300 = _____

6. Explain how you would find the answer to 6 × 29. _____

   _____
   _____

VIEWING AND DRAWING 3-D   DAB • Grade 3 • Unit 18 **261**

Discovery Assignment Book - page 261

Discovery Assignment Book (p. 261)

Home Practice*

Part 3

1. **A.** inches or centimeters

   B. square inches or square centimeters

   C. cubic inches or cubic centimeters

2. 18 cubic units

3. Answers will vary. Two possible answers are shown.

| 1 | 2 | 3 |
| 4 | 8 | |

| 3 | 3 | 3 |
| 3 | 3 | 3 |

---

*Answers for all the Home Practice in the *Discovery Assignment Book* are at the end of the unit.

Lesson 4

Top, Front, and Right Side Views

Lesson Overview

Estimated Class Sessions

2

Students view cube models from the top, front, and right side and record these three views. Students also solve puzzles that give one or more model views, a volume, a height, or a floor plan by building the appropriate cube model.

Key Content

- Identifying the same cube model from different perspectives.
- Using a grid to record the top, front, and right side views of a cube model.
- Solving problems that have multiple solutions.
- Solving open-response problems.

Key Vocabulary

- front view
- right side view
- top view

Math Facts

DPP item G provides computation and mental math practice. Bit I provides practice with the multiplication facts for the square numbers.

Homework

1. Assign the *Three Ways to Show 3-D Models* Assessment Pages either for homework or in-class assessment.
2. Assign Home Practice Part 4.

Assessment

1. Students complete the *Three Ways to Show 3-D Models* Assessment Blackline Masters.
2. Use the *Observational Assessment Record* to record students' abilities to identify the front, right, and top views of a cube model.

Materials List

Supplies and Copies

Student	Teacher
Supplies for Each Student • 30 connecting cubes • masking tape, optional	**Supplies**
Copies • 2 copies of *3 × 3 Cube Model Plans* per student (*Unit Resource Guide* Page 55) • 1 copy of *Three Ways to Show 3-D Models* per student (*Unit Resource Guide* Pages 67–68) • 2 copies of *Three-view Records* per student (*Unit Resource Guide* Page 69)	**Copies/Transparencies**

All blackline masters including assessment, transparency, and DPP masters are also on the Teacher Resource CD.

Student Books

Top, Front, and Right Side Views (*Student Guide* Pages 277–281)

Daily Practice and Problems and Home Practice

DPP items G–J (*Unit Resource Guide* Pages 17–19)
Home Practice Part 4 (*Discovery Assignment Book* Page 261)

Note: Classrooms whose pacing differs significantly from the suggested pacing of the units should use the Math Facts Calendar in Section 4 of the *Facts Resource Guide* to ensure students receive the complete math facts program.

Assessment Tools

Observational Assessment Record (*Unit Resource Guide* Pages 11–12)

Daily Practice and Problems

Suggestions for using the DPPs are on page 65.

G. Bit: Quick Addition (URG p. 17)

Do these problems in your head.
Write only the answers.

1. $5 + 6 =$
2. $50 + 60 =$
3. $60 + 40 =$
4. $60 + 30 =$
5. $40 + 70 =$
6. $20 + 80 =$

I. Bit: More Squares (URG p. 18)

For each problem the numbers in the squares must be the same.

A. $64 = \square \times \square$

B. $36 = \square \times \square$

C. $9 = \square \times \square$

D. $25 = \square \times \square$

E. $49 = \square \times \square$

F. $81 = \square \times \square$

G. $100 = \square \times \square$

H. $16 = \square \times \square$

I. $4 = \square \times \square$

J. $1 = \square \times \square$

H. Task: Joe and Moe Smart
(URG p. 18)

Joe Smart's answer for the problem 19×6 was 126. Moe Smart got a different answer. Joe said, "Well, first I did 20×6." Moe said, "I agree with that but . . ."

1. Finish Moe's statement explaining to Joe what he did wrong.
2. Tell how you can find 29×3.

J. Task: Multiplication (URG p. 19)

A. $3 \times 25 =$

B. $3 \times 24 =$

C. $3 \times 26 =$

D. $5 \times 30 =$

E. $5 \times 29 =$

F. $5 \times 31 =$

G. $4 \times 50 =$

H. $4 \times 49 =$

I. $4 \times 59 =$

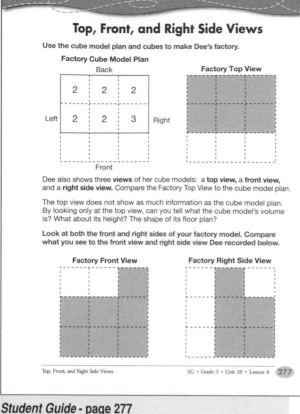

Top, Front, and Right Side Views

Use the cube model plan and cubes to make Dee's factory.

Factory Cube Model Plan

Back

2	2	2
2	2	3

Left ⟷ Right

Front

Factory Top View

Dee also shows three **views** of her cube models: a **top view**, a **front view**, and a **right side view**. Compare the Factory Top View to the cube model plan.

The top view does not show as much information as the cube model plan. By looking only at the top view, can you tell what the cube model's volume is? What about its height? The shape of its floor plan?

Look at both the front and right sides of your factory model. Compare what you see to the front view and right side view Dee recorded below.

Factory Front View   **Factory Right Side View**

Student Guide - page 277

TIMS Tip

You might write "front" and "right" on masking tape along the side of the model to keep track of the sides while the model is on the projector. As they work, students might find this helpful as well. Or remind them to refer to the cube model plan or drawing they were given in the *Student Guide* if they lose track of the sides.

Teaching the Activity

In the *Top, Front, and Right Side Views* Activity Pages in the *Student Guide,* students compare a top view of the factory model to its cube model plan. In the previous activity, students worked with cube model plans representing cube models as seen from above. Discuss the difference between the cube model plans and the top view. Guide students to see that if you shade over the numbered squares in a cube model plan you have the top view. In other words, the top view still tells you how many columns you need to build, but it does not tell you the number of cubes in each column. Therefore, the area and shape of the model's base can be found from a top view, but it provides no information about the volume or the height of the cube model.

Continuing in the *Student Guide,* students look at the factory model from the front and the right side and compare what they see to the views recorded. Make sure students position themselves so that the model is at eye level. Comparing the front view of a cube model to its shadow when placed on an overhead projector might also be helpful. Place the factory model on the overhead projector so that the front of the model faces up, as shown in Figure 10. (The outline or shadow may appear fuzzy on taller cube models.) The shadow projected on the screen will correspond to the front view. You can turn the model so that the right side faces up and the right side view is projected on the screen. Compare the shadows to the views recorded in the *Student Guide.*

 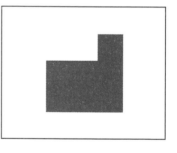

Place the model on the overhead projector with the front side facing up.

The projector will show the front view.

Figure 10: *Showing views on the overhead projector*

As students begin to record their views of cube models, it is important that they learn how to position themselves and the cube model so that they see *only* the side they are representing. Stress the importance of holding the model at eye level and keeping track of the sides appropriately.

On the second page of the *Top, Front, and Right Side Views* Activity Pages, students are given three views of a new cube model, the "house with garage." Students must build the model, look at it from the three views, and then decide which of the views presented are top, front, and right side. Once the class identifies A as the right side view, B as the front view, and C as the top view, ask,

- *Which view is the same shape as the cube model plan?* (The cube model plan, which represents a bird's-eye view, shows the top view.)

Next, on the *Top, Front, and Right Side Views* Activity Pages, a cube model plan and right view of the hotel is provided, a model Tonya made for Dee. Dee thinks Tonya's right side view is incorrect. The basis of the disagreement brings up an interesting point about views. Should only the right-most cubes be recorded in a right view or the cubes that are the highest and the widest anywhere in the model? Students are asked to build the model and to check its projection on the overhead. Dee is correct because her right side view records the highest and widest points. Tonya is incorrect because her right side view shows only the right-most cubes.

Hotel Cube Model

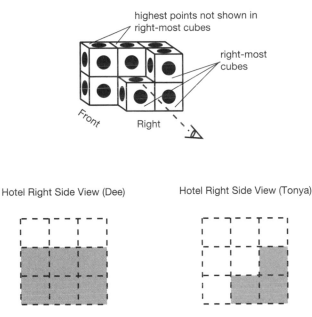

Dee's right view is correct.   Tonya's right view is incorrect.

Figure 11: *A right-hand perspective and the right side view of the hotel*

For **Questions 1–4** in the *Student Guide*, students build cube models based on the cube model plans provided. Then they record the top, front, and right side views on a copy of *Three-view Records*

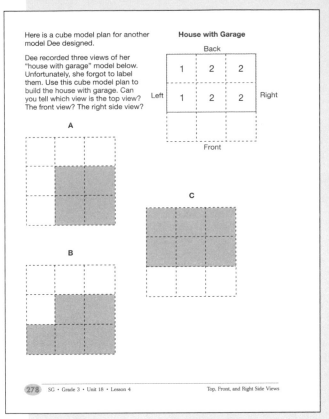

Student Guide - page 278

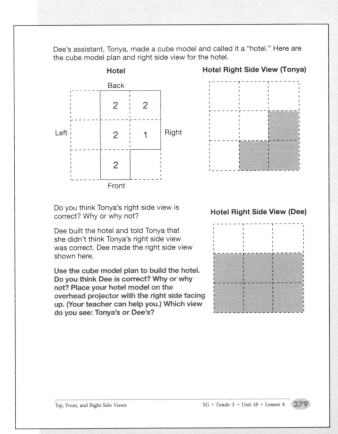

Student Guide - page 279

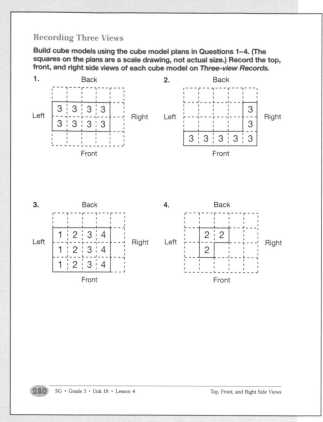

Student Guide - page 280 (Answers on p. 70)

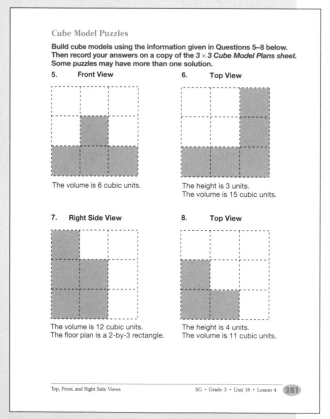

Student Guide - page 281 (Answers on p. 71)

Blackline Master. When students initially look at the top of the cube model in **Question 3,** they may have a difficult time describing what they see. Remind them that the top view is the same shape and size as the cube model plan.

In **Question 4** the front side view of the cube model is the same as the right side view. Like Tonya, some students might be tempted to record only the front-most or right-most cubes. Building the cube model in **Question 4** and projecting the three views on the overhead will help you guide a discussion about why the two views are the same.

In **Questions 5–8,** students are given one view of a cube model and some additional information, such as the volume, height, or base area of the model. Students must build a model that fits this description and then record their answers as a cube model plan. To record their answers, each student needs two copies of *3 × 3 Cube Model Plans* Blackline Master. (Some questions have multiple solutions.) You might want to build the first model together.

In the students' earlier discussion of the problem with Tonya's right side view of the hotel, they learned that a view records the highest and widest points as viewed from the top, front, or right side. Translating from views to cube models provides the opportunity for students to apply this knowledge in reverse.

Question 5, for example, provides a front view and a volume of 6 cubic units. Many answers are possible, three of which are shown in Figure 12. The variation occurs because the front view does not necessarily represent only the front-most cubes. As students discuss their answers to these questions, you can review how views are recorded.

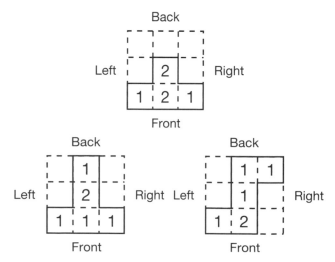

Figure 12: *Three of the many possible answers for **Question 5***

Math Facts

DPP Bit G provides practice with addition facts using mental math. Bit I provides practice with the multiplication facts for the square numbers.

Homework and Practice

- Use the *Three Ways to Show 3-D Models* Assessment Pages, described below, for either homework or assessment.

- For Task H, students find and explain an error in a computation. Task J provides multiplication practice and builds mental math skills.

- Part 4 of the Home Practice builds number sense and mental math skills by skip counting and multiplying with ending zeros.

Answers for Part 4 of the Home Practice are in the Answer Key at the end of this lesson and at the end of this unit.

Assessment

- The *Three Ways to Show 3-D Models* Assessment Pages tie together the first three activities in this unit. These pages include problems about the three different two-dimensional representations of cube models students have learned: drawings, cube model plans, and views. Students are asked to build the models to answer **Question 1.** Encourage them, however, to build the models for **Questions 2–3** as well. Each student will need 30 connecting cubes to complete the assessment.

- Use the *Observational Assessment Record* to note students' abilities to identify and describe the front, right, and top views of a cube model.

Extension

Ask students to find all solutions to **Questions 6** and **8** in the *Student Guide* and to explain how they know they have found all solutions. There is one solution to **Question 6** and three solutions to **Question 8.**

Literature Connection

- Adkins, Jan. *How a House Happens*. Walker and Company, Inc., New York, 1972.

The book shows how an architect designs a house. The top and side views are referred to as plans and elevations. Illustrations show these views and use customary measures.

Name _____ Date _____

PART 3

1. What units can be used to measure:
   A. the length of your finger? _____
   B. the area of your hand? _____
   C. the volume of a cereal box? _____

2. What is the volume of the cube model which is built using this plan?

   _____

4	3	4
2	1	4

3. Make a different cube model plan on a sheet of paper. Keep the volume the same as in Question 2. You may change the floor plan.

PART 4

1. Skip count by fives backwards from 80. Record the numbers below as you say them.

   _____
   _____

2. Skip count by fours backwards from 60. Record the numbers.

   _____
   _____

3. 6 × 3 = _____   4. 6 × 30 = _____   5. 6 × 300 = _____

6. Explain how you would find the answer to 6 × 29. _____
   _____
   _____

VIEWING AND DRAWING 3-D   DAB • Grade 3 • Unit 18 **261**

Discovery Assignment Book - page 261 *(Answers on p. 71)*

At a Glance

Math Facts and Daily Practice and Problems

DPP items G, H, and J provide computation and mental math practice. Bit I provides practice for the multiplication facts for the square numbers.

Teaching the Activity

1. On the *Top, Front, and Side Views* Activity Pages in the *Student Guide*, students compare a top view of the factory model to its cube model plan.
2. Students look at the factory model from the front and right side and compare what they see to the views recorded.
3. Place the factory model on the overhead projector. Compare the shadows to the views recorded in the *Student Guide*.
4. Students build the house with garage model.
5. Students look at the model from three views and decide which view is the top, which the front, and which the right side.
6. Students build a hotel model from a cube model plan and check its projection on the overhead. They discuss whether Tonya's or Dee's right view is correct.
7. For *Questions 1–4,* students build cube models based on the cube model plans provided. They record the top, front, and right side views on copies of *Three-view Records* Blackline Master.
8. For *Questions 5–8* in the Cube Model Puzzles section, students build models that fit given criteria and record their answers as cube model plans on copies of *3 × 3 Cube Model Plans* Blackline Master.

Homework

1. Assign the *Three Ways to Show 3-D Models* Assessment Pages either for homework or in-class assessment.
2. Assign Home Practice Part 4.

Assessment

1. Students complete the *Three Ways to Show 3-D Models* Assessment Blackline Masters.
2. Use the *Observational Assessment Record* to record students' abilities to identify the front, right, and top views of a cube model.

Extension

Have students find all the possible solutions for *Questions 6* and *8.*

Connection

How a House Happens by Jan Adkins shows how an architect designs a house.

Answer Key is on pages 70–72.

Notes:

Three Ways to Show 3-D Models

1. Here are some 3-D drawings. Build each cube model, and find the area of its base, its volume, and its height.

A.

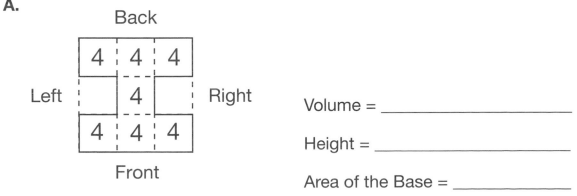

Model A

1 cubic unit

Volume = _____

Height = _____

Area of the Base = _____

B.

Model B

Volume = _____

Height = _____

Area of the Base = _____

2. Here are some cube model plans. Provide the missing information.

A.

Back

4	4	4
	4	
4	4	4

Left   Right

Front

Volume = _____

Height = _____

Area of the Base = _____

B.

Back

5	4	
	3	2
		1

Left   Right

Front

Volume = _____

Height = _____

Area of the Base = _____

3. Here is a cube model plan. Provide the Top View, Front View, and Right Side View.

Back

3	3	3
3	3	3

Left   Right

Front

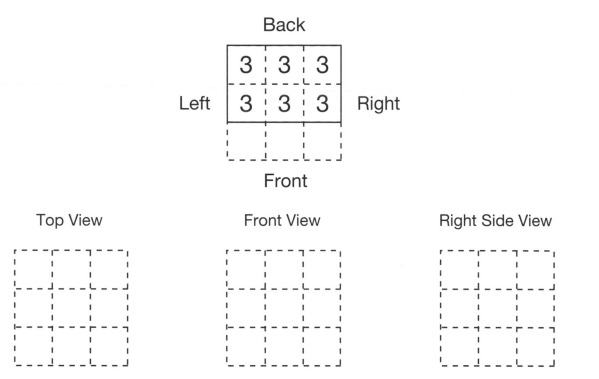

Top View   Front View   Right Side View

Assessment Blackline Master

Three-view Records

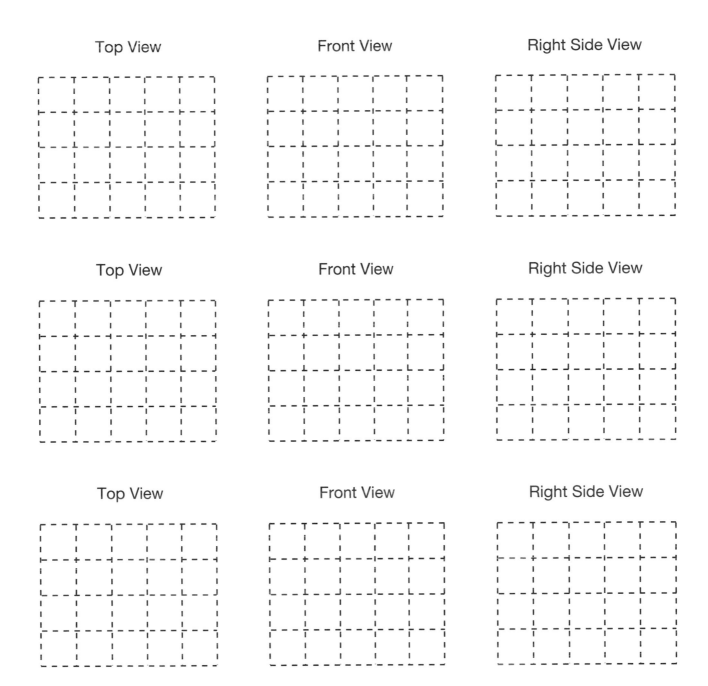

Top View   Front View   Right Side View

Top View   Front View   Right Side View

Top View   Front View   Right Side View

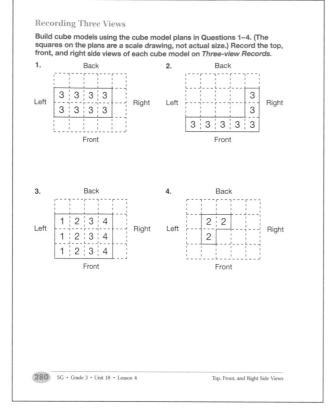

Student Guide (p. 280)

1.
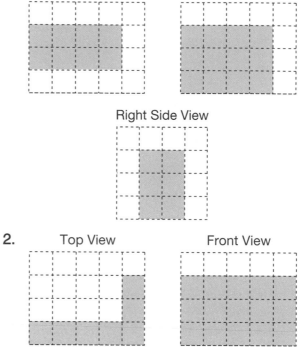

2.
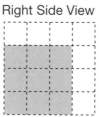

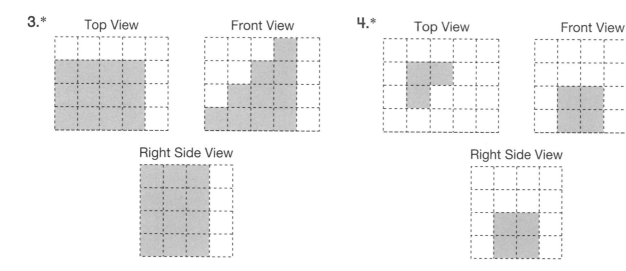

*Answers and/or discussion are included in the Lesson Guide.

Student Guide (p. 281)

5. Answers will vary. Here is one example.*

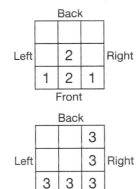

6.

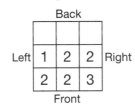

7. Answers will vary. However, keep in mind that the floor plan needs to be a 2 × 3 rectangle.

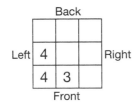

8. Answers will vary. Here is one example.

	Back	
Left 4		Right
4	3	
	Front	

Discovery Assignment Book (p. 261)

Home Practice†

Part 4

1. 80, 75, 70, 65, ... , 15, 10, 5, 0

2. 60, 56, 52, 48, 44, 40, 36, 32, 28, 24, 20, 16, 12, 8, 4, 0

3. 18

4. 180

5. 1800

6. Solution strategies will vary. You could subtract 6 from 6 × 30. 180 − 6 = 174

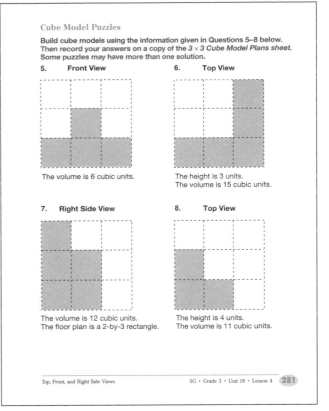

Student Guide - page 281

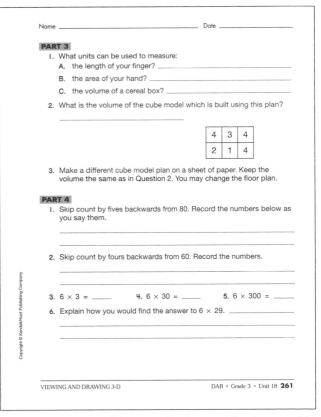

Discovery Assignment Book - page 261

*Answers and/or discussion are included in the Lesson Guide.
†Answers for all the Home Practice in the *Discovery Assignment Book* are at the end of the unit.

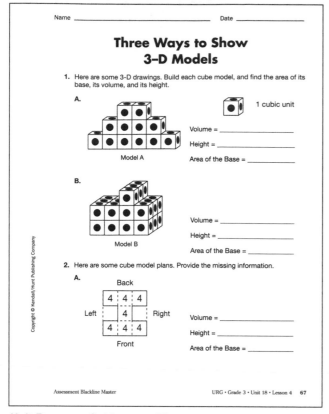

Unit Resource Guide - page 67

Unit Resource Guide (p. 67)

Three Ways to Show 3-D Models

1. **A.** Volume = 12 cu units

   Height = 3 units

   Area of the Base 5 = sq units

   B. Volume = 27 cu units

   Height = 3 units

   Area of the Base = 12 sq units

2. **A.** Volume = 28 cu units

   Height = 4 units

   Area of the Base = 7 sq units

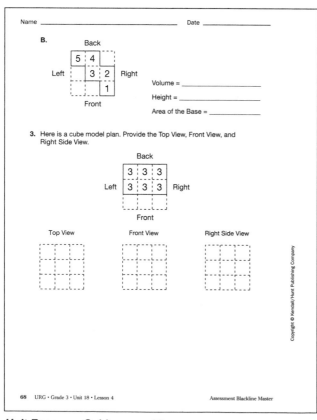

Unit Resource Guide - page 68

Unit Resource Guide (p. 68)

   B. Volume = 15 cu units

   Height = 5 units

   Area of the Base = 5 sq units

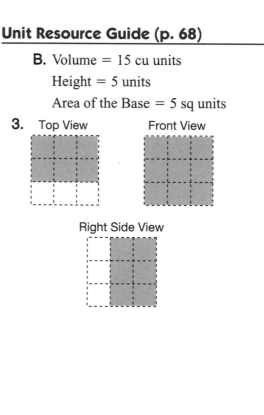

Lesson 5

Problems with Shapes

Estimated Class Sessions

1

Lesson Overview

This lesson is a series of problems that build on the activities in this unit. Students draw a three-dimensional figure and answer questions about a cube model when given its cube model plan.

Key Content

- Finding the area of the base, height, and volume of a cube model.
- Translating between a cube model and its cube model plan.
- Identifying the properties of a rectangular prism.
- Solving multistep word problems.

Math Facts

DPP Bit K is the multiplication quiz on the square numbers.

Homework

Assign some or all of the problems for homework.

Assessment

1. Students complete DPP item K Multiplication Quiz: Squares.
2. Use the *Observational Assessment Record* to document students' abilities to find the area of the base, height, and volume of a cube model.
3. Transfer appropriate documentation from the Unit 18 *Observational Assessment Record* to students' *Individual Assessment Record Sheets*.

Materials List

Supplies and Copies

Student	Teacher
Supplies for Each Student • 20 connecting cubes • crayons or colored pencils	**Supplies**
Copies • 1 copy of *3 × 3 Cube Model Plans* per student (*Unit Resource Guide* Page 55)	**Copies/Transparencies**

All blackline masters including assessment, transparency, and DPP masters are also on the Teacher Resource CD

Student Books
Problems with Shapes (*Student Guide* Pages 282–283)

Daily Practice and Problems and Home Practice
DPP items K–L (*Unit Resource Guide* Pages 19–20)

Note: Classrooms whose pacing differs significantly from the suggested pacing of the units should use the Math Facts Calendar in Section 4 of the *Facts Resource Guide* to ensure students receive the complete math facts program.

Assessment Tools
Observational Assessment Record (*Unit Resource Guide* Pages 11–12)
Individual Assessment Record Sheet (*Teacher Implementation Guide,* Assessment section)

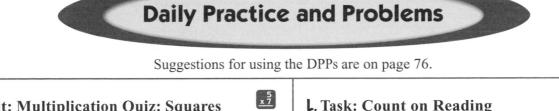

Daily Practice and Problems

Suggestions for using the DPPs are on page 76.

K. Bit: Multiplication Quiz: Squares
(URG p. 19)

Do these problems in your head.
Write only the answers.

A. $5 \times 5 =$	B. $4 \times 4 =$
C. $9 \times 9 =$	D. $7 \times 7 =$
E. $10 \times 10 =$	F. $8 \times 8 =$
G. $3 \times 3 =$	H. $1 \times 1 =$
I. $6 \times 6 =$	J. $2 \times 2 =$

L. Task: Count on Reading
(URG p. 20)

Ms. Ropel's class read for a total of 778 minutes. Mrs. Cob's class read for 976 minutes.

1. How many more minutes did Mrs. Cob's class read than Ms. Ropel's?

2. A. Did Mrs. Cob's class read for longer than ten hours?

   B. Explain how you can change the answer to Question 1 to hours and minutes.

3. How many minutes altogether did the two classes read?

Teaching the Activity

The problems in this lesson strengthen spatial visualization skills and understanding of geometric terms and concepts. In *Questions 1–4,* students draw a rectangular prism and identify the faces, edges, and vertices. In *Questions 5–7,* they find the area of the base, height, and volume of a cube model by looking at the cube model plan. For *Question 8,* students add on to an existing cube model according to written specifications. They will need a copy of the *3 × 3 Cube Model Plans* Blackline Master from Lesson 3. Encourage students to use connecting cubes to answer these questions.

Using the Problems. Students can work on the problem individually, in pairs, or in groups. One approach is to ask students to work on the problems individually and then to come together in pairs or small groups to compare solutions. Then the group's solutions can be shared with others in a class discussion. Assign some or all of the problems for homework as appropriate throughout the unit.

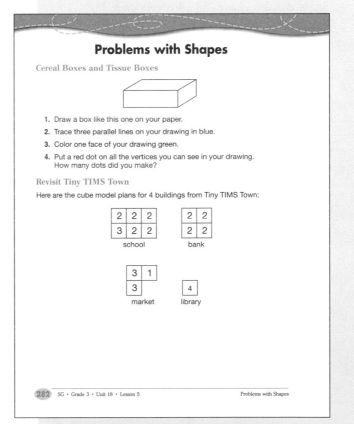

Student Guide - page 282 (Answers on p. 78)

5. Which building has the largest volume?

6. Which building has the smallest volume?

7. What is the area of the base of each building?

8. The market is planning to expand so that the floor plan will look like this:

There is a height limit of 4 units in Tiny TIMS Town. The market owners want to double the volume of their store using this floor plan. Draw cube model plans to show two ways they could expand the market.

Student Guide - page 283 *(Answers on p. 78)*

Homework and Practice

- DPP Task L provides practice with computation and converting minutes to hours.

- Assign some or all of the problems in the *Student Guide* for homework.

Assessment

- DPP Bit K is the Multiplication Quiz: Squares and assesses the multiplication facts for the square numbers.

- Use the *Observational Assessment Record* to note students' abilities to find the area of the base, height, and volume of cube models.

- Transfer appropriate documentation from the Unit 18 *Observational Assessment Record* to students' *Individual Assessment Record Sheets.*

At a Glance

Math Facts and Daily Practice and Problems

DPP Bit K is the multiplication quiz on the square numbers. Task L is a word problem involving computation and time.

Teaching the Activity

1. Students solve the word problems on the *Problems with Shapes* Activity Pages in the *Student Guide*.
2. Students discuss solutions and solution strategies.

Homework

Assign some or all of the problems for homework.

Assessment

1. Students complete DPP item K Multiplication Quiz: Squares.
2. Use the *Observational Assessment Record* to document students' abilities to find the area of the base, height, and volume of a cube model.
3. Transfer appropriate documentation from the Unit 18 *Observational Assessment Record* to students' *Individual Assessment Record Sheets.*

Answer Key is on page 78.

Notes:

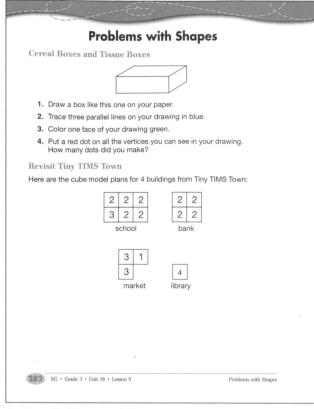

Problems with Shapes

Cereal Boxes and Tissue Boxes

1. Draw a box like this one on your paper.
2. Trace three parallel lines on your drawing in blue.
3. Color one face of your drawing green.
4. Put a red dot on all the vertices you can see in your drawing. How many dots did you make?

Revisit Tiny TIMS Town

Here are the cube model plans for 4 buildings from Tiny TIMS Town:

2	2	2
3	2	2

school

2	2
2	2

bank

3	1
3	

market

4

library

Student Guide - page 282

Student Guide (p. 282)

Problems with Shapes

1.–3. Answers will vary. Here is an example drawing. There are three sets of three parallel line segments—a horizontal set, a vertical set, and an oblique set.

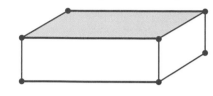

4. 7 dots

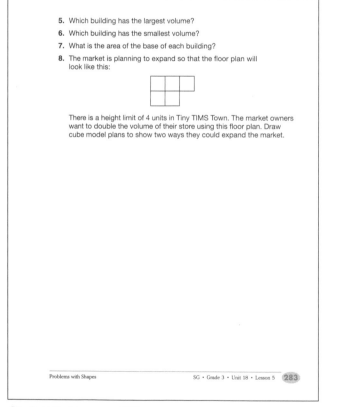

5. Which building has the largest volume?
6. Which building has the smallest volume?
7. What is the area of the base of each building?
8. The market is planning to expand so that the floor plan will look like this:

There is a height limit of 4 units in Tiny TIMS Town. The market owners want to double the volume of their store using this floor plan. Draw cube model plans to show two ways they could expand the market.

Student Guide - page 283

Student Guide (p. 283)

5. the school
6. the library
7. school: 6 square cm; bank: 4 square cm; market: 3 square cm; library: 1 square cm
8. Answers will vary. The volume should be 14 square cm. Two possible answers are shown.

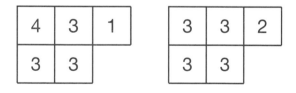

4	3	1
3	3	

3	3	2
3	3	

Discovery Assignment Book (p. 260)

Part 1

1. 60
2. 20
3. 40
4. 45
5. 120
6. 54
7. 99 pounds
   (350 lbs − 183 lbs = 167 lbs.
   167 − 68 lbs = 99 lbs)

Part 2

1. 1600
2. 1700
3. 1500
4. 1601
5. 1700
6. 1523
7. Possible strategy:
   $800 + 2 + 700 + 99 = 800 + 700 + 101 = 1601$
8. 193 miles

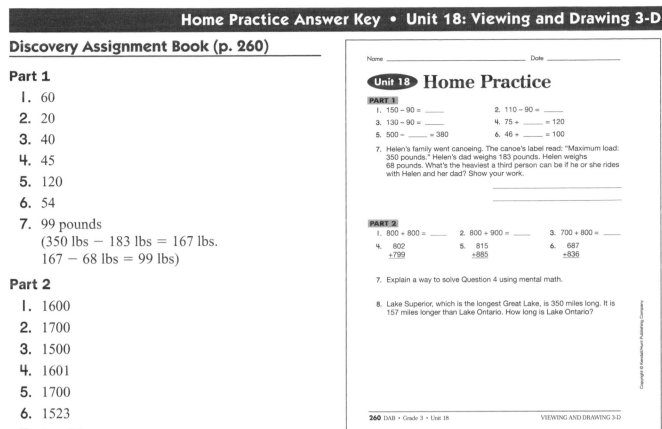

Discovery Assignment Book - page 260

Name _____ Date _____

PART 3

1. What units can be used to measure:
   A. the length of your finger? _____
   B. the area of your hand? _____
   C. the volume of a cereal box? _____

2. What is the volume of the cube model which is built using this plan?

   _____

4	3	4
2	1	4

3. Make a different cube model plan on a sheet of paper. Keep the volume the same as in Question 2. You may change the floor plan.

PART 4

1. Skip count by fives backwards from 80. Record the numbers below as you say them.

   _____
   _____

2. Skip count by fours backwards from 60. Record the numbers.

   _____
   _____

3. $6 \times 3 =$ _____   4. $6 \times 30 =$ _____   5. $6 \times 300 =$ _____

6. Explain how you would find the answer to 6×29. _____
   _____
   _____

VIEWING AND DRAWING 3-D   DAB • Grade 3 • Unit 18 **261**

Copyright © Kendall/Hunt Publishing Company

Discovery Assignment Book - page 261

Discovery Assignment Book (p. 261)

Part 3

1. A. inches or centimeters

   B. square inches or square centimeters

   C. cubic inches or cubic centimeters

2. 18 cubic units

3. Answers will vary. Two possible answers are shown.

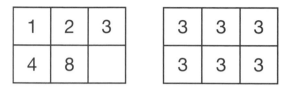

1	2	3
4	8	

3	3	3
3	3	3

Part 4

1. 80, 75, 70, 65, ... , 15, 10, 5, 0

2. 60, 56, 52, 48, 44, 40, 36, 32, 28, 24, 20, 16, 12, 8, 4, 0

3. 18

4. 180

5. 1800

6. Solution strategies will vary. You could subtract 6 from 6×30. $180 - 6 = 174$

Glossary

This glossary provides definitions of key vocabulary terms in the Grade 3 lessons. Locations of key vocabulary terms in the curriculum are included with each definition. Components Key: URG = *Unit Resource Guide,* SG = *Student Guide,* and DAB = *Discovery Assignment Book.*

A

Area (URG Unit 5; SG Unit 5)
The area of a shape is the amount of space it covers, measured in square units.

Array (URG Unit 7 & Unit 11)
An array is an arrangement of elements into a rectangular pattern of (horizontal) rows and (vertical) columns. (*See* column and row.)

Associative Property of Addition (URG Unit 2)
For any three numbers a, b, and c we have $a + (b + c) = (a + b) + c$. For example in finding the sum of 4, 8, and 2, one can compute $4 + 8$ first and then add 2: $(4 + 8) + 2 = 14$. Alternatively, we can compute $8 + 2$ and then add the result to 4: $4 + (8 + 2) = 4 + 10 = 14$.

Average (URG Unit 5)
A number that can be used to represent a typical value in a set of data. (*See also* mean and median.)

Axes (URG Unit 8; SG Unit 8)
Reference lines on a graph. In the Cartesian coordinate system, the axes are two perpendicular lines that meet at the origin. The singular of axes is axis.

B

Base (of a cube model) (URG Unit 18; SG Unit 18)
The part of a cube model that sits on the "ground."

Base-Ten Board (URG Unit 4)
A tool to help children organize base-ten pieces when they are representing numbers.

Base-Ten Pieces (URG Unit 4; SG Unit 4)
A set of manipulatives used to model our number system as shown in the figure at the right. Note that a skinny is made of 10 bits, a flat is made of 100 bits, and a pack is made of 1000 bits.

Base-Ten Shorthand (SG Unit 4)
A pictorial representation of the base-ten pieces as shown.

Nickname	Picture	Shorthand
bit		·
skinny		/
flat		
pack		

Best-Fit Line (URG Unit 9; SG Unit 9; DAB Unit 9)
The line that comes closest to the most number of points on a point graph.

Bit (URG Unit 4; SG Unit 4)
A cube that measures 1 cm on each edge. It is the smallest of the base-ten pieces that is often used to represent 1. (*See also* base-ten pieces.)

C

Capacity (URG Unit 16)
1. The volume of the inside of a container.
2. The largest volume a container can hold.

Cartesian Coordinate System (URG Unit 8)
A method of locating points on a flat surface by means of numbers. This method is named after its originator, René Descartes. (*See also* coordinates.)

Centimeter (cm)
A unit of measure in the metric system equal to one-hundredth of a meter. (1 inch = 2.54 cm)

Column (URG Unit 11)
In an array, the objects lined up vertically.

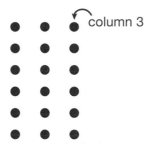
column 3

Common Fraction (URG Unit 15)
Any fraction that is written with a numerator and denominator that are whole numbers. For example, $\frac{3}{4}$ and $\frac{9}{4}$ are both common fractions. (*See also* decimal fraction.)

Commutative Property of Addition (URG Unit 2 & Unit 11)
This is also known as the Order Property of Addition. Changing the order of the addends does not change the sum. For example, $3 + 5 = 5 + 3 = 8$. Using variables, $n + m = m + n$.

Commutative Property of Multiplication (URG Unit 11)
Changing the order of the factors in a multiplication problem does not change the result, e.g., $7 \times 3 = 3 \times 7 = 21$. (*See also* turn-around facts.)

Congruent (URG Unit 12 & Unit 17; SG Unit 12)
Figures with the same shape and size.

Convenient Number (URG Unit 6)
A number used in computation that is close enough to give a good estimate, but is also easy to compute mentally, e.g., 25 and 30 are convenient numbers for 27.

Coordinates (URG Unit 8; SG Unit 8)
An ordered pair of numbers that locates points on a flat surface by giving distances from a pair of coordinate axes. For example, if a point has coordinates (4, 5) it is 4 units from the vertical axis and 5 units from the horizontal axis.

Counting Back (URG Unit 2)
A strategy for subtracting in which students start from a larger number and then count down until the number is reached. For example, to solve $8 - 3$, begin with 8 and count down three, 7, 6, 5.

Counting Down (*See* counting back.)

Counting Up (URG Unit 2)
A strategy for subtraction in which the student starts at the lower number and counts on to the higher number. For example, to solve $8 - 5$, the student starts at 5 and counts up three numbers (6, 7, 8). So $8 - 5 = 3$.

Cube (SG Unit 18)
A three-dimensional shape with six congruent square faces.

Cubic Centimeter (cc)
(URG Unit 16; SG Unit 16)
The volume of a cube that is one centimeter long on each edge.

1 cm
1 cm
1 cm
cubic centimeter

Cup (URG Unit 16)
A unit of volume equal to 8 fluid ounces, one-half pint.

D

Decimal Fraction (URG Unit 15)
A fraction written as a decimal. For example, 0.75 and 0.4 are decimal fractions and $\frac{75}{100}$ and $\frac{4}{10}$ are called common fractions. (*See also* fraction.)

Denominator (URG Unit 13)
The number below the line in a fraction. The denominator indicates the number of equal parts in which the unit whole is divided. For example, the 5 is the denominator in the fraction $\frac{2}{5}$. In this case the unit whole is divided into five equal parts.

Density (URG Unit 16)
The ratio of an object's mass to its volume.

Difference (URG Unit 2)
The answer to a subtraction problem.

Dissection (URG Unit 12 & Unit 17)
Cutting or decomposing a geometric shape into smaller shapes that cover it exactly.

Distributive Property of Multiplication over Addition (URG Unit 19)
For any three numbers a, b, and c, $a \times (b + c) = a \times b + a \times c$. The distributive property is the foundation for most methods of multidigit multiplication. For example, $9 \times (17) = 9 \times (10 + 7) = 9 \times 10 + 9 \times 7 = 90 + 63 = 153$.

E

Equal-Arm Balance
See two-pan balance.

Equilateral Triangle (URG Unit 7)
A triangle with all sides of equal length and all angles of equal measure.

Equivalent Fractions (SG Unit 17)
Fractions that have the same value, e.g., $\frac{2}{4} = \frac{1}{2}$.

Estimate (URG Unit 5 & Unit 6)
1. (verb) To find *about* how many.
2. (noun) An approximate number.

Extrapolation (URG Unit 7)
Using patterns in data to make predictions or to estimate values that lie beyond the range of values in the set of data.

F

Fact Family (URG Unit 11; SG Unit 11)
Related math facts, e.g., $3 \times 4 = 12$, $4 \times 3 = 12$, $12 \div 3 = 4$, $12 \div 4 = 3$.

Factor (URG Unit 11; SG Unit 11)
1. In a multiplication problem, the numbers that are multiplied together. In the problem $3 \times 4 = 12$, 3 and 4 are the factors.
2. Whole numbers that can be multiplied together to get a number. That is, numbers that divide a number evenly, e.g., 1, 2, 3, 4, 6, and 12 are all the factors of 12.

Fewest Pieces Rule (URG Unit 4 & Unit 6; SG Unit 4)
Using the least number of base-ten pieces to represent a number. (*See also* base-ten pieces.)

Flat (URG Unit 4; SG Unit 4)
A block that measures 1 cm $\times$ 10 cm $\times$ 10 cm. It is one of the base-ten pieces that is often used to represent 100. (*See also* base-ten pieces.)

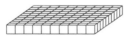

Flip (URG Unit 12)
A motion of the plane in which a figure is reflected over a line so that any point and its image are the same distance from the line.

Fraction (URG Unit 15)
A number that can be written as $\frac{a}{b}$ where a and b are whole numbers and b is not zero. For example, $\frac{1}{2}$, 0.5, and 2 are all fractions since 0.5 can be written as $\frac{5}{10}$ and 2 can be written as $\frac{2}{1}$.

Front-End Estimation (URG Unit 6)
Estimation by looking at the left-most digit.

G

Gallon (gal) (URG Unit 16)
A unit of volume equal to four quarts.

Gram
The basic unit used to measure mass.

H

Hexagon (SG Unit 12)
A six-sided polygon.

Horizontal Axis (SG Unit 1)
In a coordinate grid, the *x*-axis. The axis that extends from left to right.

I

Interpolation (URG Unit 7)
Making predictions or estimating values that lie between data points in a set of data.

J

K

Kilogram
1000 grams.

L

Likely Event (SG Unit 1)
An event that has a high probability of occurring.

Line of Symmetry (URG Unit 12)
A line is a line of symmetry for a plane figure if, when the figure is folded along this line, the two parts match exactly.

Line Symmetry (URG Unit 12; SG Unit 12)
A figure has line symmetry if it has at least one line of symmetry.

Liter (l) (URG Unit 16; SG Unit 16)
Metric unit used to measure volume. A liter is a little more than a quart.

M

Magic Square (URG Unit 2)
A square array of digits in which the sums of the rows, columns, and main diagonals are the same.

Making a Ten (URG Unit 2)
Strategies for addition and subtraction that make use of knowing the sums to ten. For example, knowing $6 + 4 = 10$ can be helpful in finding $10 - 6 = 4$ and $11 - 6 = 5$.

Mass (URG Unit 9 & Unit 16; SG Unit 9)
The amount of matter in an object.

Mean (URG Unit 5)
An average of a set of numbers that is found by adding the values of the data and dividing by the number of values.

Measurement Division (URG Unit 7)
Division as equal grouping. The total number of objects and the number of objects in each group are known. The number of groups is the unknown. For example, tulip bulbs come in packages of 8. If 216 bulbs are sold, how many packages are sold?

Measurement Error (URG Unit 9)
The unavoidable error that occurs due to the limitations inherent to any measurement instrument.

Median (URG Unit 5; DAB Unit 5)
For a set with an odd number of data arranged in order, it is the middle number. For an even number of data arranged in order, it is the number halfway between the two middle numbers.

Meniscus (URG Unit 16; SG Unit 16)
The curved surface formed when a liquid creeps up the side of a container (for example, a graduated cylinder).

Meter (m)
The standard unit of length measure in the metric system. One meter is approximately 39 inches.

Milliliter (ml) (URG Unit 16; SG Unit 16)
A measure of capacity in the metric system that is the volume of a cube that is one centimeter long on each edge.

Multiple (URG Unit 3 & Unit 11)
A number is a multiple of another number if it is evenly divisible by that number. For example, 12 is a multiple of 2 since 2 divides 12 evenly.

N

Numerator (URG Unit 13)
The number written above the line in a fraction. For example, the 2 is the numerator in the fraction $\frac{2}{5}$. (*See also* denominator.)

O

One-Dimensional Object (URG Unit 18; SG Unit 18)
An object is one-dimensional if it is made up of pieces of lines and curves.

Ordered Pairs (URG Unit 8)
A pair of numbers that gives the coordinates of a point on a grid in relation to the origin. The horizontal coordinate is given first; the vertical coordinate is given second. For example, the ordered pair (5, 3) tells us to move five units to the right of the origin and 3 units up.

Origin (URG Unit 8)
The point at which the *x*- and *y*-axes (horizontal and vertical axes) intersect on a coordinate plane. The origin is described by the ordered pair (0, 0) and serves as a reference point so that all the points on the plane can be located by ordered pairs.

P

Pack (URG Unit 4; SG Unit 4)
A cube that measures 10 cm on each edge. It is one of the base-ten pieces that is often used to represent 1000. (*See also* base-ten pieces.)

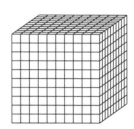

Palindrome (URG Unit 6)
A number, word, or phrase that reads the same forward and backward, e.g., 12321.

Parallel Lines (URG Unit 18)
Lines that are in the same direction. In the plane, parallel lines are lines that do not intersect.

Parallelogram (URG Unit 18)
A quadrilateral with two pairs of parallel sides.

Partitive Division (URG Unit 7)
Division as equal sharing. The total number of objects and the number of groups are known. The number of objects in each group is the unknown. For example, Frank has 144 marbles that he divides equally into 6 groups. How many marbles are in each group?

Pentagon (SG Unit 12)
A five-sided, five-angled polygon.

Perimeter (URG Unit 7; DAB Unit 7)
The distance around a two-dimensional shape.

Pint (URG Unit 16)
A unit of volume measure equal to 16 fluid ounces, i.e., two cups.

Polygon
A two-dimensional connected figure made of line segments in which each endpoint of every side meets with an endpoint of exactly one other side.

Population (URG Unit 1; SG Unit 1)
A collection of persons or things whose properties will be analyzed in a survey or experiment.

Prediction (SG Unit 1)
Using data to declare or foretell what is likely to occur.

Prime Number (URG Unit 11)
A number that has exactly two factors. For example, 7 has exactly two distinct factors, 1 and 7.

Prism
A three-dimensional figure that has two congruent faces, called bases, that are parallel to each other, and all other faces are parallelograms.

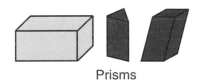
Prisms

Not a prism

Product (URG Unit 11; SG Unit 11; DAB Unit 11)
The answer to a multiplication problem. In the problem $3 \times 4 = 12$, 12 is the product.

Q

Quadrilateral (URG Unit 18)
A polygon with four sides.

Quart (URG Unit 16)
A unit of volume equal to 32 fluid ounces; one quarter of a gallon.

R

Recording Sheet (URG Unit 4)
A place value chart used for addition and subtraction problems.

Rectangular Prism (URG Unit 18; SG Unit 18)
A prism whose bases are rectangles. A right rectangular prism is a prism having all faces rectangles.

Regular (URG Unit 7; DAB Unit 7)
A polygon is regular if all sides are of equal length and all angles are equal.

Remainder (URG Unit 7)
Something that remains or is left after a division problem. The portion of the dividend that is not evenly divisible by the divisor, e.g., $16 \div 5 = 3$ with 1 as a remainder.

Right Angle (SG Unit 12)
An angle that measures 90°.

Rotation (turn) (URG Unit 12)
A transformation (motion) in which a figure is turned a specified angle and direction around a point.

Row (URG Unit 11)
In an array, the objects lined up horizontally.

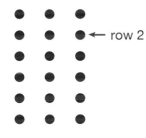

Rubric (URG Unit 2)
A written guideline for assigning scores to student work, for the purpose of assessment.

S

Sample (URG Unit 1; SG Unit 1)
A part or subset of a population.

Skinny (URG Unit 4; SG Unit 4)
A block that measures 1 cm $\times$ 1 cm $\times$ 10 cm. It is one of the base-ten pieces that is often used to represent 10. (*See also* base-ten pieces.)

Square Centimeter (sq cm) (SG Unit 5)
The area of a square that is 1 cm long on each side.

Square Number (SG Unit 11)
A number that is the product of a whole number multiplied by itself. For example, 25 is a square number since $5 \times 5 = 25$. A square number can be represented by a square array with the same number of rows as columns. A square array for 25 has 5 rows of 5 objects in each row or 25 total objects.

Standard Masses
A set of objects with convenient masses, usually 1 g, 10 g, 100 g, etc.

Sum (URG Unit 2; SG Unit 2)
The answer to an addition problem.

Survey (URG Unit 14; SG Unit 14)
An investigation conducted by collecting data from a sample of a population and then analyzing it. Usually surveys are used to make predictions about the entire population.

T

Tangrams (SG Unit 12)
A type of geometric puzzle. A shape is given and it must be covered exactly with seven standard shapes called tans.

Thinking Addition (URG Unit 2)
A strategy for subtraction that uses a related addition problem. For example, $15 - 7 = 8$ because $8 + 7 = 15$.

Three-Dimensional (URG Unit 18; SG Unit 18)
Existing in three-dimensional space; having length, width, and depth.

TIMS Laboratory Method (URG Unit 1; SG Unit 1)
A method that students use to organize experiments and investigations. It involves four components: draw, collect, graph, and explore. It is a way to help students learn about the scientific method.

Turn (URG Unit 12)
(*See* rotation.)

Turn-Around Facts (URG Unit 2 & Unit 11 p. 37; SG Unit 11)
Addition facts that have the same addends but in a different order, e.g., $3 + 4 = 7$ and $4 + 3 = 7$. (*See also* commutative property of addition and commutative property of multiplication.)

Two-Dimensional (URG Unit 18; SG Unit 18)
Existing in the plane; having length and width.

Two-Pan Balance
A device for measuring the mass of an object by balancing the object against a number of standard masses (usually multiples of 1 unit, 10 units, and 100 units, etc.).

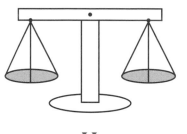

U

Unit (of measurement) (URG Unit 18)
A precisely fixed quantity used to measure. For example, centimeter, foot, kilogram, and quart are units of measurement.

Using a Ten (URG Unit 2)
1. A strategy for addition that uses partitions of the number 10. For example, one can find $8 + 6$ by thinking $8 + 6 = 8 + 2 + 4 = 10 + 4 = 14$.
2. A strategy for subtraction that uses facts that involve subtracting 10. For example, students can use $17 - 10 = 7$ to learn the "close fact" $17 - 9 = 8$.

Using Doubles (URG Unit 2)
Strategies for addition and subtraction that use knowing doubles. For example, one can find $7 + 8$ by thinking $7 + 8 = 7 + 7 + 1 = 14 + 1 = 15$. Knowing $7 + 7 = 14$ can be helpful in finding $14 - 7 = 7$ and $14 - 8 = 6$.

V

Value (URG Unit 1; SG Unit 1)
The possible outcomes of a variable. For example, red, green, and blue are possible values for the variable *color*. Two meters and 1.65 meters are possible values for the variable *length*.

Variable (URG Unit 1; SG Unit 1)
1. An attribute or quantity that changes or varies.
2. A symbol that can stand for a variable.

Vertex (URG Unit 12; SG Unit 12)
1. A point where the sides of a polygon meet.
2. A point where the edges of a three-dimensional object meet.

Vertical Axis (SG Unit 1)
In a coordinate grid, the y-axis. It is perpendicular to the horizontal axis.

Volume (URG Unit 16; SG Unit 16)
The measure of the amount of space occupied by an object.

Volume by Displacement (URG Unit 16)
A way of measuring volume of an object by measuring the amount of water (or some other fluid) it displaces.

W

Weight (URG Unit 9)
A measure of the pull of gravity on an object. One unit for measuring weight is the pound.

X

Y

Z